CELTIC TREE OGHAM

© Giacomo Tosti

About the Author

Sharlyn Hidalgo has an MA in psychology, and although she is now in semiretirement, she is a practicing astrologer, tarot reader, teacher, healer, artist, and author. She taught school for twenty-five years, teaching every grade from kindergarten on up to the community college level. She has worked as a mental health counselor for an agency and in private practice.

Because of her Celtic roots and her love for trees, she is enamored with the ancient spiritual practices of the British Isles. She is author of *The Healing Power of Trees: Spiritual Journeys through the Celtic Tree Calendar* and *Celtic Tree Rituals: Ceremonies for the Thirteen Moon Months and A Day*, published by Llewellyn Worldwide, and a tree card deck titled *Celtic Tree Oracle*, through Blue Angel Publishing (illustrated by Jimmy Manton).

Sharlyn teaches classes on the Celtic trees, runs a yearly Druid apprenticeship, and holds ceremonies that celebrate the turning of the wheel in the Celtic native European tradition. She offers Tree Readings in which she tunes into a chosen tree and shares its message with her client. She also teaches classes on tarot, astrology, mandalas, and creativity. As a ceremonialist and circle leader, she is dedicated to protecting nature and promoting peace and healing on our planet.

Through Nicki Scully, Sharlyn is certified as a practitioner and teacher of Alchemical Healing, which is a shamanistic and energetic healing form sourced in Egypt. Sharlyn has been to Egypt eight times and led three successful tours in Egypt. She has written a book about her experience there titled *Nazmy: Love Is My Religion: Egypt, Travel, and a Quest for Peace* with a foreword by Jean Houston. She teaches classes on the Egyptian Mysteries. She just published her first novel titled *The Pharaoh's Daughter: A Spiritual Sojourn: The Healing Power of Past, Present, and Future Lives in Egypt*.

Sharlyn lives in Seattle, Washington, and is happily married with two grown children. She can be found online at www.alchemicalhealingarts.com and www.alchemicalhealingarts.blogspot.com.

RITUALS AND TEACHINGS
OF THE AICME AILIM
VOWELS AND THE FORFEDA

CELTIC TREE OGHAM

SHARLYN HIDALGO

Llewellyn Publications
Woodbury, Minnesota

First Edition
First Printing, 2021

Book format by Samantha Peterson
Cover design by Shira Atakpu
Cover illustration by Meraylah Allwood
Illustrations on page 23 and 36 by Llewellyn Art Department
Interior tree illustrations by Meraylah Allwood

Llewellyn Publications is a registered trademark of Llewellyn Worldwide Ltd.

Library of Congress Cataloging-in-Publication Data
Names: Hidalgo, Sharlyn, author.
Title: Celtic tree ogham : rituals and teachings of the aicme ailim vowels and the forfeda / by Sharlyn Hidalgo.
Description: First edition. | Woodbury, MN : Llewellyn Worldwide, Ltd, 2021. | Includes bibliographical references. | Summary: "This easy-to-follow guide shows you how to build a deeper connection to nature as you learn about the aicme ailim vowels and the forfeda" — Provided by publisher.
Identifiers: LCCN 2021036840 (print) | LCCN 2021036841 (ebook) | ISBN 9780738768298 | ISBN 9780738768403 (ebook)
Subjects: LCSH: Celts—Religion. | Tree worship. | Ogham alphabet. | Ritual. | Rites and ceremonies.
Classification: LCC BL900 .H53 2021 (print) | LCC BL900 (ebook) | DDC 299/.16138—dc23
LC record available at https://lccn.loc.gov/2021036840
LC ebook record available at https://lccn.loc.gov/2021036841

Llewellyn Worldwide Ltd. does not participate in, endorse, or have any authority or responsibility concerning private business transactions between our authors and the public.
All mail addressed to the author is forwarded but the publisher cannot, unless specifically instructed by the author, give out an address or phone number.
Any internet references contained in this work are current at publication time, but the publisher cannot guarantee that a specific location will continue to be maintained. Please refer to the publisher's website for links to authors' websites and other sources.

Llewellyn Publications
A Division of Llewellyn Worldwide Ltd.
2143 Wooddale Drive
Woodbury, MN 55125-2989
www.llewellyn.com

Printed in the United States of America

Other Books by Sharlyn Hidalgo

The Healing Power of Trees
Celtic Tree Oracle
Celtic Tree Rituals
Nazmy: Love Is My Religion
The Pharaoh's Daughter

I dedicate this book to seekers everywhere. It is my hope that you will find the spiritual path that feeds you that leads you to your spiritual home. Know that there is no right way to walk in the light, and that your true nature is spirit and knows no limitation. Know that while you walk on this earth, in this dimension you are nature itself, and you are free to commune with the spirits of the flora and the fauna as well as the totems, deities, and guides that live in higher dimensions and your loved ones and ancestors that have crossed over the veil.

I dedicate this book to the trees and their wisdom teaching. Without their healing messages, I would not be the person that I am today. I honor the wisdom keepers on the planet.

I thank my husband, Ricardo Hidalgo, for his support, and my children, Eli Ross and Rianna Louise, for their solid love.

I thank all of my students for teaching me more than I taught them and for playing with me as I led them in ceremony and taught classes, not knowing at first if these would be helpful or meaningful.

I am grateful to my relatives and ancestors who herald from the British Isles and for these teachings that have traveled through time and hold nature as sacred. I am grateful for the land, the water, the air, the sea, and this Celtic body of wisdom that teaches reverence and respect for the natural world and for the forests—for all the ecosystems that we rely on.

CONTENTS

UILLEAND · HONEYSUCKLE
147

PHAGOS · BEECH
159

MOR · SEA
175

INTRODUCTION

I began my study of Celtic teachings over twenty-five years ago, when I was looking to reconnect with the ancient spirituality of Pagan people in the British Isles before Christianity's influence. It is interesting to note that there was no internet at that time; information had to come from books, and there were few books available on these teachings. This did not deter me as I began this work in an effort to discover my roots.

I can trace my heritage to Wales, Cornwall, and central England. I also have ancestors from the Isle of Man, Ireland, and Scotland. Over the years, I have spent hundreds of hours studying Celtic teachings, and I admit that I have fallen in love with Celtic wisdom. And the good news is that now, there are many more books available on the subject, as well as websites that the reader can review.

Unfortunately, the Celts did not write down their history. It was passed on by word of mouth and memorized songs and folklore. One has to sift through myths, legends, and even fairy tales to discover the greater truths and spiritual beliefs of the Celts. There are only bits and pieces of information, but this limited information provided a rich foundation for many modern spiritual practices like Druidism, Wicca, Celtic shamanism, Celtic faery spirituality, Celtic Christianity, Celtic reconstructionism, and the Grail tradition. I am sure there are others I do not know about!

Throughout my studies, it became clear that the ancient teachings of the British Isles are all about human connection to nature and nature's mysticism. Celtic wisdom teaches that we are surrounded by the magic of many worlds and that our ancestors are close by and do assist us. We can communicate with ancestors and loved ones that have crossed over and receive their loving support and guidance. We can also communicate with the totems, guides, and deities in the unseen world. This is our birthright, and the Celts understood that this communication is meant to help us live well and in harmony with all life on the planet.

Modern humans have access to a multitude of folktales, legends, and lore that depict a mythology that is steeped in magic from all over the British Isles. Celtic attitudes and beliefs show us how to be good stewards of the land and how to show respect for the wisdom in each rock, animal, plant, and body of water upon Mother Earth. There is also wisdom to be found in the sun, moon, stars, and imaginal realm. Ancient Celts revered the wisdom of the trees, springs, wells, mountains, and land. They respected nature and its cycles. They believed in the ability to see into the unseen and to return with healing and wisdom. In fact, wisdom exudes from the land, from the sea, and from the air. The Celts knew that there were doorways into new truths and other worlds. I am grateful for this body of knowledge, which is called *Celticity*. Celticity is an essential way to keep your connection to your own wild self alive and well.

My love of the Celtic tree alphabet and its modern use as a teaching tool has only grown with time. After years of leading ceremonies and writing about Celtic teachings, the Celtic tree alphabet (known as the Ogham) and the Celtic tree calendar have become the center of my spiritual practice. I have written about that practice in two other books.[1] My first book, *The Healing Power of Trees: Spiritual Journeys through the Celtic Tree Calendar*, came out in 2010 and provides a good description of each of the twenty-five ogham. In 2019, Llewellyn published my second book, *Celtic Tree Rituals: Ceremonies for the Thirteen Moon Months and a Day*, which has a ceremony and a personal story for the first fifteen ogham that make up Celtic tree calendar. My purpose in writing these books was to offer in-depth ways to interact with the teachings of the Celtic tree calendar, providing more of an experiential way to relate to the trees.

After writing extensively about the first fifteen ogham in my book *Celtic Tree Rituals*, it feels important to me to make sure that all twenty-five fews of the Ogham get their own time in the sun. This book is about the last ten ogham of the Celtic tree alphabet, which include the five vowels that make up the *aicme ailim* fews and the last five fews, called the *forfeda*. Each few of the Ogham alphabet represents a sound, a letter, and, usually, a tree teaching or a nature teaching. If you love trees, enjoy Celtic teachings, and honor nature, I hope this is a book you will enjoy.

It is also my hope that this book will allow you to make relationships with the Silver Fir and Pine, the Gorse, the Heather and Mistletoe, the White Poplar and Aspen, the Yew, the Grove (any group of trees growing in a forest, an orchard, wild areas, a local park, or your own backyard), the Spindle, the Honeysuckle, the Beech, and the last ogham, Mor, the Sea, which represents our links to our homelands, our mothers, and the Great Mother herself. I am hopeful that you will be able to work with these trees and symbols and their wisdom. They have powerful teachings and healings that can be added to the teachings found in the Celtic tree calendar.

---

1. I have also published the *Celtic Tree Oracle* deck. I think these cards are a worthwhile addition to your library if you are intent on learning about the Celtic trees and using them in your practice.

The Ogham tree alphabet that I use has twenty-five symbols and letters that correspond to a tree or other plant, with some exceptions. These symbols and letters have a host of ideas and spiritual meanings—teachings, if you will—that relate to the Celtic cosmology. You will discover that each of the themes in the alphabet is tied to ancient Celtic culture and mythology. You will also discover that these teachings are relevant to your own modern life.

Almost everything about the Ogham is under dispute, and the tree calendar and its origins have long been a source of controversy among Celtic scholars. However, many modern Pagans feel that the information within the alphabet and the calendar predate the time of Druidic influence over Celtic religious matters. They believe that this knowledge was long a part of the nature-loving spirituality of the ancient people of the British Isles and was kept alive and passed down through songs, stories, and poems, all memorized. Memorization was at the heart of the passing down of these teachings and of folklore through the ages.

Many practicing Pagans are happy to work with the magical properties of the trees. Thus, the Ogham has emerged as a powerful modern-day oracle. It has become a valid tool for today's spiritual seekers. Many Pagans and Wiccans have taken to using the Ogham as a divination system and a body of wisdom, and they can attest to its vibrancy. In my mind, the age and origin of this body of knowledge is less important than the application of the symbols and the value that they impart to spiritual growth today.

In This Book

Within the pages of this book, you will become familiar with the Ogham and the tree correspondences that make up the Celtic tree calendar. I explain these in detail in chapter 1. In this introduction, you will find a brief presentation about each of the last ten ogham, a section about how to use this book, why this book is relevant for the times we live in, and a bit about me and my work with the Celtic tree Ogham.

Each of the last ten ogham presented here has a chapter that opens with the ogham and the letter or letters it represents; the corresponding tree, plant, or element of nature; keywords; totems; guides and deities; practical guidance; and more specific information about the tree. In each chapter, I have created a ceremony that honors that ogham. Ceremonies include teachings, a meditation, and suggested songs, chants, and activities. Each chapter ends with a story that shares my experience interacting with the energy and teaching of that ogham. Finally, the chapter offers some practical ideas for how you can interact with its ogham.

Please note that some of the totems, guides, and deities that I have included are modern additions to the teachings. From time to time, I use other mystery school totems, guides, and deities. They became part of my practice when I opened myself up to the energies of the ceremonies throughout the years. Egyptian, Norse, Native American, Greek, Roman, and other influences have shown up. I believe they add richness to the medicine that we are creating with the Ogham. When I talk about a deity from another culture, a parenthetical notation will indicate that deity's culture. (I also identify which part of the British Isles a god or goddess comes from in parentheses.) I hope I do not ruffle any feathers for not sticking strictly to Celtic mythology and knowledge. If it is bothersome to you, simply substitute a Celtic totem, guide, or deity that you are familiar with.

Connecting to the Trees

I know from my own experiences that the energies and healing teachings of the trees will communicate with you. All you have to do is ask and offer them your interest and attention. The trees are readily accessible. If you close your eyes and imagine a particular tree, it will be there. The more time you spend communicating with the trees, the better relationship you establish. This is how you create a better connection for receiving their wisdom, healing, and magic.

I invite you to trust dreams, intuitions, yearnings, synchronicities and serendipity, visions, daydreams, and your inner guidance. Listen for that quiet voice within. There are many ways that the spirit world will reach out to you once it knows you are eager to communicate and learn. Take note of books, movies, people, and events that attract you. These can act as guideposts along the way. Use meditation, guided journeying, and creativity as a means of connecting to Source wisdom. Create art, write poems and prose, keep a journal, write songs, play music, move, sing—allow the creative spirit to dance through you. Pay attention to bodily symptoms and ask specific symptoms for their messages.

The tree spirits and their wisdom and knowledge are eager to connect with you. Ask the totems, guides, and deities for their help. Guidance, healing, and support are offered. Humans live in a paradise of beauty, mystery, and magic, and there are doorways between worlds to ensure communication. This communication can strengthen character, lead you through dark times, encourage you in your goals and aspirations, and support you as you become a better steward for Mother Earth.

We are capable of creating a living alchemy that moves us beyond our restrictive or dysfunctional family backgrounds, narrow cultural and religious teachings, and limited beliefs and opinions. We can strive to discipline and curb our negative tendencies and allow the expression of greater understanding and more love, acceptance, and light. It is our job to foster healing and forgiveness. The teaching of the trees asks us to observe Mother Nature and rest in her cycles, but we must heal and protect her as well.

How to Use This Book

I have included ceremonies throughout this book. When I first began my study of the Ogham, I did solitary ceremonies. I gathered leaves, cones, and fallen limbs or branches from the tree I was focusing on and made an altar in my home. I tried to find each tree I was working with so I could spend time with it in my yard, neighborhood, or local parks. (I live in Seattle, so finding these trees was not a hard thing to do.) If you don't have a wealth of trees to visit in person, the internet is the way to go. I read what I could to familiarize myself with the tree's teaching and made a little ceremony to honor it. I looked at pictures of the tree. I developed prayers and gave gratitude for the tree's wisdom. I worked with its totems, guides, and deities.

All the ceremonies in this book are written for group work, but they can be altered and done solo. Read through the chapter you want to work with and pick and choose what parts of the ceremony are workable for you. Adapt the ceremonies as you see fit. Record the guided meditations and play them back during your personal ceremony. Play around with singing and drumming. Play music you enjoy. Write in your journal. If you plan to do all of the ceremonies by yourself, have a special journal that you keep just for ceremony and tree teachings.

Familiarize yourself with songs that tie into the tree's teachings. I make some musical suggestions, but you can choose any songs that connect you to the theme. This can be a fun and creative way to add to your ceremony. Sing and drum solo at first to gain confidence. It takes time to feel comfortable singing and drumming for others. When I first began a women's circle years ago, we were quite timid, but with time we became robust drummers and singers, and this only added to the atmosphere of our rituals.

The aicme ailim can be thought of as the seasonal trees. Two trees are found to represent the winter. Pine begins the cycle of these seasonal ogham, follows the Winter Solstice, and carries us into the new year. You can begin your study on New Year's Day with the Ailim/ Silver Fir or Pine if you so desire. This is the first tree of the aicme ailim, which represents the vowels. Then you can move on to the Gorse and the spring, the Heather and Mistletoe in the summer, the Poplar or Aspen in the fall, and finally the Yew, which comes before the Winter Solstice and ends the cycle. In this way, you progress through the seasons of the year as you study these ogham.

Then there are the last five ogham, called the forfeda. These last five ogham offer us additional wisdom. Although the Koad/Grove represents one date, "The Day," October 31, its meaning is to remind us to take time out of our busy lives for spiritual renewal and reflection. Oir/Spindle, Uilleand/Honeysuckle, Phagos/Beech, and Mor/ the Sea are not associated with a time of the year and can be studied at any time for their particular teachings and wisdom. However, I do tend to focus on each of these seasonally to make sure that I include them in my teachings. The Spindle is taught around the time of Imbolc, Honeysuckle is given to the time around Beltane, Beech to Lammas, and Mor is usually taught in late summer, early fall, or as the last ogham of the teaching or studying schedule.

You can choose to move through the book as the ogham are listed and proceed with the teachings and ceremonies. You would study the vowels first, then move to the teachings of the forfeda. Perhaps you would like to work through the Wheel of the Year and take the whole year to interact with these ten ogham. You could choose to read and do the ceremonies close to the sabbats as a way to keep the teachings in a workable order. Here is a list of how you would follow those through the year:

- A/Ailim/Silver Fir/Pine: After the Winter Solstice

- Oi/Oir/Spindle: Around Imbolc

- O/Ohn/Gorse: Around the Spring Equinox

- Ui/Uilleand/Honeysuckle: Around Beltane
- U/Ur/Heather and Mistletoe: Around the Summer Solstice
- Io/Phagos/Beech: Around Lammas, Lughnassad
- E/Eadha/White Poplar/Aspen: Around Fall Equinox
- Ea/Koad/Grove/The Day: Around Samhain
- I/Ioho/Yew: After Samhain and up to the Winter Solstice
- Ae/Mor/Sea: Can go with the summer or fall, or at the end of your year of study

Or you can work with a particular ogham because you are called to its themes and teachings. Your goal is to make relationships with each tree (or the Grove or the Sea). When you've finished working with an ogham, let your studies culminate in a modified ceremony for solo use or by inviting a few friends to share in a ceremony.

The phenomenal healing power I have witnessed in the teachings of the trees, which shows up for folks in ceremony, meditation, and journeying, has left me in awe time after time. Divinity cannot be found in dogma. It shows up through the magical, the mystical, and the unexplained, and it is simply beautiful. It is to be experienced. All you need to do is extend the invitation, set up your protections (which communicate respect), open to the energy, and make some time, whether this is individually or with a group. It is important to have an intention, ask for permission, and ask for the help that you require, and always remember gratitude. It is my aim to provide you with pathways into your own experience.

It is also important to give back in some way. You can lend support to a community project that plants trees, take care of your own trees, or lend financial support to worthy tree projects. I especially like an organization called TreeSisters. You can find them on Facebook or on their website at www.treesisters.org.

The Importance of the Ogham

The gifts of Celtic symbolism and mythology—which come through in the tree teachings of the tree calendar and Ogham alphabet—have a profound connection to the natural world and to the Mysteries. Celtic symbolism and mythology have fostered in me a deeper connection to nature and have provided important and meaningful guidance. I follow the teachings of the trees and Celtic wisdom within the form of the alphabet, which is the foundation of my practice. I find that working with the wisdom of the Ogham keeps me close to nature. By following the sequence of the tree teachings each month, I have come to be a better steward of the planet and a more conscious human.

I find that the cyclical nature of the tree teachings is organic and reliable, and that the alphabet and the calendar provide a meaningful doorway into Celtic cosmology. I believe it provides a powerful structure for today's seekers. Many Goddess worshippers, Neopagans, Wiccans, tree lovers, and native European spiritualists have based their spiritual practice upon these teachings. These teachings from the past can help us live in a more sacred way and be better stewards of our planet.

We are living in strange and stressful times. I believe these teachings can only help us. There is wisdom to help us develop our courage and resolve. Without the trees, we cannot live. I ask that we protect them. I hope their teachings can turn those who choose to read this book toward a more ecological perspective and lifestyle. Thank the Goddess for our indigenous cultures that based their economies and structures upon the principles that honored life through the practice of harmonious living with animals, water, soil, plant life, the elements, and the cosmos, none of us separate within the web of life. The ancient ones and our ancestors are still with us, as are their teachings and practices. Nature still provides for us. I share these ancient teachings from the British Isles to encourage you to wake up to your true nature and to your role in the greater scheme of life.

Tree lore from the British Isles is thought to be a powerful school of knowledge passed on from the ancient people of that land. I am not interested so much in the history of the alphabet or the calendar (scarce as it is); I am moved by the power of its teaching. I know in my bones that its information is sourced in ancient knowledge that was passed on orally and was lost to us—and yet has reawakened, like a phoenix. I value tree teachings as they help tie me to the British Isles and my ancestry. They also tie me to the land where I live now. Most importantly, they teach me to pay attention to seasonal changes and the cycles of time with gratitude. They teach me to be respectful and to live as lightly as I can on the earth. The work I share here is born out of my own personal immersion into these mysteries. I have taken the information and made it my own. I hope it can be useful to you.

For me, the knowledge of the ancient Celts feeds and informs my modern practice as a doorway to wisdom. Hopefully, this book can be your doorway into these sacred teachings. Thank you for opening yourself up to the tree teachings and their healing power. This spiritual practice, which moves you through the cyclical changes of the seasons and the years, will surely enhance your own spiritual practice and connection to all that is.

THE OGHAM

The Celtic tree Ogham is a mnemonic device as well as a magical system. Its documented origins are at least seventeen hundred years old. The term *Ogham* (pronounced "oh-am" or "ohm") is used to refer collectively to the twenty-five letters or symbols, also known as *fews*, that make up the Celtic tree alphabet. Each letter refers to a specific tree, shrub, vine, or reed (with the exception of the twenty-fifth letter, which represents the sea) in the version of the alphabet that I use. It is thought that these symbols were used as mnemonic devices for learning and remembering the letters and sounds that they represented.

The Celtic tree alphabet, known as the Ogham, is an ancient Irish alphabet. It was mainly used to write Primitive and Old Irish, as well as to write Old Welsh, Pictish, and Latin. It can be found inscribed on stone cairns throughout Ireland and in England, Scotland, Wales, and the Isle of Man. This early medieval alphabet was used primarily to write Primitive Irish. Its letters appear on monumental inscriptions in this classical Ogham, dating from the fourth to the sixth century CE.

After the conversion to Christianity in the fifth century, Old Irish began to appear as glosses (notes written in the margins) and other margin writings in Latin manuscripts, beginning in the sixth century. This Old Irish is referred to as *scholastic Ogham*, and it dates from the sixth to the ninth century CE.

Much of our present-day knowledge of the Ogham comes from *The Book of Ballymote*, which was compiled in the fourteenth century and is a collection of older manuscripts and documents. These early manuscripts, such as *The Book of Lecan* (1416), *The Book of Lismore* (late fourteenth/early fifteenth century), and *The Book of Leinster* (twelfth century) mention the Ogham and are manuscript collections of prose and poetry.[2] Another important writing is *The Ogam Tract*, or *In Lebor Ogaim*, which is found in fourteenth-century manuscripts and sixteenth-century texts as well as *The Scholars' Primer*.[3]

George Calder, a lecturer in Celtic studies at the University of Glasgow, published a book in 1917 titled *Auraicept na n'Eces*, or *The Scholars' Primer*, which transcribed this early material.[4] This book includes the texts of *The Ogam Tract* from *The Book of Ballymote* and *The Yellow Book of Lecan*, as well as the text of the *Trefhocul* from *The Book of Leinster*. This material was recorded as early as the seventh century by scholars and is also found in twelfth-century and fourteenth-century manuscripts, which were compiled from earlier texts and oral records. Sadly, there just isn't much information that has survived, and the Ogham's use and meanings are obscure. I am grateful that we do have these fourteenth-century fragments, the later sixteenth-century texts, and Calder's transcriptions.

The alphabet itself is made up of symbols consisting of straight lines, which were traditionally etched upon sticks or stones. Each symbol represents a particular letter or letter combination. These can be written vertically (usually read from bottom to top) or horizontally (usually read from left to right), with an arrow or some other kind of marking indicating where to begin reading. The markings are made along a stem line called the *druim*, which means "the whale's backbone."

---

2. Kynes, *Whispers from the Woods*, 41.

3. Forest, *Celtic Tree Magic*, 10.

4. Murray and Murray, *Celtic Tree Oracle*, 16.

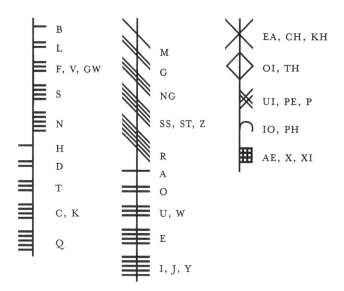

Besides its mundane uses to mark boundaries and name places, it is thought that the Ogham was used to indicate ideas and beliefs related to ancient Celtic cosmology and philosophy. Although this alphabet was not used for writing or speech as we know it, the ogham markings were often scratched on stones or wooden staves, which were then used as oracles for divination.

There are reports that the Ogham was used to write ancient stories and sagas. These texts were said to have existed before Christianity. In order to transcribe their stories and sagas, it is thought that the Celts incised letters on bark or wands of hazel and aspen. These were called the Rods of Fili and were kept in special libraries. Due to the passage of time, we now only have carved stones and various medieval manuscripts that verify the existence of the Ogham. As to its origins, no one can say for sure.

Groups of the Ogham

Presented as a whole, the Celtic Ogham is arranged in five groups of five letters. The first twenty letters are called the *feada* (FEHD-uh) and are the original characters. These first four groups are referred to as the *aicme*, meaning "tribes," and they probably represented Ireland's provinces.

Each of the aicmes has its own name. The first group of five letters is called the *aicme beith*; the second five, the *aicme hauthe*; and the third five, the *aicme muin*. The aicme beith, aicme hauthe, and aicme muin represent the Ogham's consonants. The next five letters are the vowels; they are known as the *aicme ailim*. (Refer to appendix B for more information about the Ogham.)

The final five letters that make up the twenty-five letters of the Ogham are thought to have been added to the alphabet later, in an effort to accommodate Greek and Latin words. They are called the *forfeda* (FOR-fehd-uh). They represent vowel combinations as well as consonant combinations. Because they are more complex, they could not have easily been carved into sticks and stone and, with a few rare exceptions, we find them mainly in early manuscripts.

The Ogham in This Book

As I mentioned in the introduction, this book will be focusing on the last ten ogham of the Celtic tree alphabet, the aicme ailim and the forfeda. Each ogham is paired with a tree, a plant, the Grove, or the Sea.

The Aicme Ailim

The aicme ailim consists of the last five of the feada, or fews. It includes Ailim, Ohn, Ur, Eadha, and Ioho. These five ogham represent the vowel sounds in the Celtic tree alphabet. The five trees that correspond with these ogham can be identified with the seasons. Two trees share the winter: one before the Winter Solstice and one after.

The Ogham symbol for the Ailim / Silver Fir or Pine represents the vowel sound A. It represents foresight, higher perspective, and a connection to the higher self and higher dimensions of love and understanding. It rules the period of wintertime *after* the solstice.

THE AICME AILIM

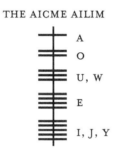

The Ogham symbol for the Ohn / Gorse represents the vowel sound O. It symbolizes collecting and gathering, community and cooperation, sweetness, and the promise of new life. It can be associated with the spring.

The Ogham symbol for the Ur / Heather and Mistletoe represents the vowel U, and the letter W could be substituted in Old Irish. It symbolizes spiritual power and healing. It can be associated with the summer.

The Ogham symbol for Eadha / Poplar or Aspen represents the vowel E. It symbolizes meeting adversity with courage. It can be associated with the fall.

The Ogham symbol for Ioho / Yew represents the vowel I. J and Y could be substituted in Old Irish. It symbolizes death and rebirth, legacies, wisdom, and the connection to our ancestors and other realms. It can be associated with the period of time after Samhain, up to and including the Winter Solstice.

The Forfeda

The forfeda is the name for the last five "extra" ogham of the tree alphabet. The forfeda represent the vowel combinations as well as consonant combinations. These ogham were probably invented in the Old Irish period, around the fourth to the sixth century. They are said to have been added to the alphabet in order to accommodate Greek and Latin. They were added after the use of Latin came to Ireland; the people using the Ogham needed other symbols for the diphthongs and extra sounds in Greek. They are also included in what is known as *The Ogam Tract*, which is found in fragments of various fourteenth-century manuscripts. This is the main source of the Bríatharogams, or the word oghams that pair an Ogham letter or sigil with a corresponding tree or plant. Hence, we come to the common title of the tree alphabet. I have also read that the forfeda may have been used as a magical alphabet in medieval times.

The forfeda in folklore are also referred to the "crane bag" and are said to be a gift from the sea god Manannán mac Lir. It was said that this crane knowledge added special significance and wisdom to the Celtic belief system. Manannán, the guardian of the afterlife known as the otherworld, was the son of the sea god Lir. Lir was part of the Tuatha Dé Danann, the supernatural race found in pre-Christian Irish mythology. Legend says that Manannán possessed a magical bag formed from the skin of a sacred crane.

There was a young woman named Aoife who was in love with Manannán's son, and she was transformed into a crane through a spell cast by a jealous rival named Iuchra. It is said that the crane lived with Manannán for 200 years, and upon her death, Manannán lovingly formed the crane bag, in which he placed his most-loved treasures.

According to the story, the bag was said to contain Manannán's shirt and knife; the belt and hook of the smith, the god Goibniu (the magical metal smith of the Tuatha Dé Danann); the shears of the King of Alban (King of Scotland); the helmet of the King of Lochlainn (a warrior king of Norse influence in Scotland, and progenitor of early kings in the Isles); a belt of the skin of a great whale (perhaps referring to the backbone of the whale, the stem line on which the Ogham letters sit); the bones of the pigs belonging to Assal (a member of the Tuatha Dé Danann who owned a magical spear and seven magical pigs that could be slain but would always reappear the next day, providing a never-ending source of sustenance); and Manannán's own house. When the tide was high, the contents of the bag were visible, but when the tide was low, they vanished.

The themes of magical appearances and disappearances, shifts in ownership, shifts in worlds, and shifts in consciousness apply to the many stories about the crane bag. The crane itself is associated with death and rebirth and the ability to travel between the worlds. Perhaps the magical bag is not a bag at all, but rather a container for the Mysteries. It represents all the realms and planes and the interconnectedness of life; it is a metaphor for unity, harmony, and the oneness that contains everything.

The crane bag contained secret contents of a magical nature that provided the owner with special power and influence. It may have originally contained all the letters of the Ogham. In that sense, the letters and alphabet represent writing and the ability to configure poetic wisdom and divination in verse. Sacred inspiration in spoken and written words could confer truth and wisdom; this could indeed provide powers and influence. I often have my students make their own crane bag and ask them to fill it with small objects of power that represent their unique skills and visions.

Today, within the Ogham that I follow, we find these items in the crane bag: the shears of the King of Scotland, the helmet of the King of Lochlainn, the bones of Assal's swine, the hook of the fierce smith

Goibniu, and the shirt of Manannán himself, representing a map of the sea showing its latitude and longitude lines.

The Ogham symbol for the Koad/Grove is the shears and represents the vowel combination Ea and the consonant combinations Ch and Kh. This ogham symbolizes the temple, the silence, the void, initiation, meditation, recommitment to the spiritual path, and communication with ancestors and loved ones who have passed on. The special day falling on October 31 is called The Day, and it is set aside for spiritual contemplation. It is the extra day that makes up the 365-day Samhain calendar, which includes the thirteen-month divisions.

The Ogham symbol for the Oir/Spindle is the helmet and it stands for the vowel combination Oi and the consonant combination Th. It represents fulfillment, insight, light, and lightning.

The Ogham symbol for the Uilleand/Honeysuckle is the cross-bones and it stands for the vowel combination Ui, the vowel combination Pe, and the consonant P. It represents secrets, seeking, and insight.

The Ogham symbol for the Phagos/Beech is the hook and it stands for the vowel combination Io and the consonant combination Ph. It represents generations, past knowledge, and the ancestors.

The Ogham symbol for Mor/the Sea is the warp and weft of the shirt. It stands for the vowel combination Ae, the consonant combination Xi, and the consonant X. It represents journeys, maternal links, mothers, and homelands. It is an ogham that can represent gratitude for our loved ones and ancestors that have passed. It reminds us to remember the homeland from which we herald as well as the spiritual teachings and knowledge of those lands. It is a symbol for the Great Mother and Mother Earth.

I see Mor as representing the end and the beginning, As the final symbol of the ogham, I picture Mor at the center of the Wheel of the Year and, in my mind, it represents our inevitable return to the invisible formless land where all things began. Mor is all about the cycles of time that we are born into, live through, and finally die in as we pass through the veil and return to the formless land of the unseen. The beginning and the end: maiden, mother, and crone.

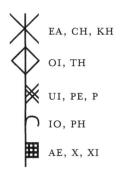

EA, CH, KH

OI, TH

UI, PE, P

IO, PH

AE, X, XI

Origins of the Ogham

The Ogham's twenty-five fews embody the wise spiritual teachings of the ancient Celts. Each few has a special teaching; it is believed that the principles of nature were separated into various wisdom teachings and placed in different trees, plants, and other elements of nature. Legend has it that these letters were inspired by Ogma, the god of eloquence, who has ties to Thoth, Hermes, and Mercury, gods of communication and writing. Ogma, a god from Irish and Scottish mythology, represents higher wisdom and intellect. He is a member of the Tuatha Dé Danann (the original magical people of Ireland). Ogma is thought to be the inventor of the Ogham, the script in which Irish Gaelic was first written.

The development of the Ogham system is usually credited to the Druids (although its origins may date back even earlier). Druids were wise elders who established powerful positions for themselves by acting as advisors to tribal leaders. They developed a significant relationship with nature. Through careful observation of nature's cycles and rhythms, they developed a unique cosmology and followed a system of ritual and ceremony that honored nature, the trees, and the movements of celestial bodies in their annual cycles. The Druids developed many techniques for divination that drew on nature itself; they used birds, trees, and the weather to divine the future. It is said that the Druids' original inspiration for the Ogham was the leg movements of cranes in flight. The Ogham itself and its special teachings and principles were taught through question and answer, then passed on through memorization.

In addition to writing the Ogham, Druids also used hand and finger movements to communicate the letters of the alphabet. The Druids had a nonverbal hand language known only to initiates, and its secrecy was possibly one way the alphabet was kept alive over time in spite of various invasions that led to the eventual repression of Pagan beliefs. The fingertips and each area above and below the finger and thumb joints represented one of the letters in the ogham. They used the fingertip of one hand to point to the different letters on the other hand. There were other forms of this communication system, known as the shinbone Ogham and the nose Ogham, in which the fingers could be placed upon the shin or nose to communicate.

The sequence of letters/trees/months that is placed upon the hands probably was used to facilitate mnemonic signing, and this follows the Birch, Rowan, Alder, Willow, and Ash sequence that I use in the Samhain system. Since Druids did not write their information down, they relied on building a system of strong memorization and mnemonic devices. Songs and poems recited over and over again also helped to maintain this system.

It is thought that hand movements were important to secret and exclusive societies in Druid or Bardic traditions because members could communicate in sign language without noninitiates even being aware that any such communication was taking place. Perhaps this was used to preserve long-lost teachings when various places within the British Isles and their Pagan beliefs were infiltrated by other groups, namely the Romans who brought Christianity.

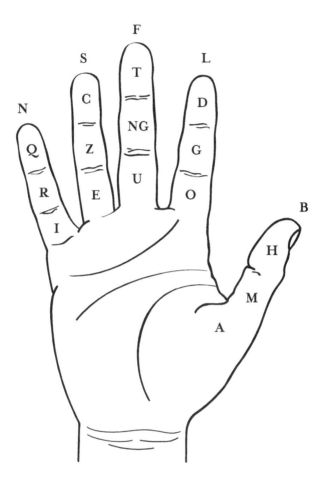

There is a historical habit of referring to the Ogham alphabet as "Beith, Luis, and Nuin," in spite of the fact that we are using the order of Beith, Luis, and Fearn. The reference could be an abbreviation for the alphabet. The reference is reinforced by the fact that the gesture of "the Horned God" (used as a greeting or recognition of initiates) uses only the thumbs, forefingers, and ring fingers, which spells out Beith, Luis, and Nuin. It is plausible that these three had been used as shorthand or as a nickname for the Druidic mysteries and teachings and were not meant to refer to the actual order of the trees as they fall within the Celtic calendar.

The Celtic Calendars

There are different Ogham and there are different tree correspondences. Please note that because there are many systems, there are different pairings for which tree goes with which ogham. Some people do not address the forfeda at all and only work with the original twenty ogham. And many people, including myself, associate the Ogham with a calendar, but this is not a requirement.

I will explain the two most common versions of the Celtic calendar. People often get very confused when they learn that there are two versions of the Celtic calendar. They learn one calendar and its dates and then they discover the other and wonder which is "right." The fact is that we cannot really know. Using the Celtic calendar as a spiritual teaching is actually a modern adaptation based on this ancient alphabet. There is definitely controversy over which system to use. I will explain which calendar I use and why to shed some light on this.

The Samhain Calendar

I get a lot of questions about the dates I use for the Celtic tree calendar. I hope this next section will clear up any confusion.

The Celtic alphabet that I use follows the order of the first fifteen ogham of the Celtic tree alphabet. It is known as the Samhain calendar. I learned about this calendar from the book *The Witch's Book of Days* and, although I was aware of the work of Robert Graves and the calendar that begins on January 24, I felt more drawn to this one.

This calendar is based upon thirteen moon divisions, all named for trees or plants, and is associated with an ogham consisting of fifteen phonetic consonant sounds. (Two months have two trees in order to fit all fifteen trees into the thirteen months.) This lunar calendar is a system of thirteen twenty-eight-day months. At the end of the last month, which is Elder, we add a day so that the calendar includes the 365 days that make up a year. Thus, October 31 is very special. It is designated as a time-out from life as usual. It is celebrated as The Day and corresponds to the Grove, which is where the ancients met in community to hold their ceremonies and commune with the Mysteries. The Celtic New Year is November 1 and corresponds with the Birch tree. I use the calendar to structure how I move through a year of spiritual practice. Here are the dates I use:

DATES	TREE(S)
October 31	The Koad/the Grove
November 1–November 28	Beith/Birch
November 29–December 26	Luis/Rowan
December 27–January 23	Fearn/Alder
January 24–February 20	Saille/Willow
February 21–March 20	Nuin/Ash
March 21–April 17	Huathe/Hawthorn
April 18–May 15	Duir/Oak
May 16–June 12	Tinne/Holly
June 13–July 10	Coll/Hazel and Quert/Apple
July 11–August 7	Muin/Vine

DATES	TREE(S)
August 8–September 4	Gort/Ivy
September 5–October 2	Ngetal/Reed and Straif/Blackthorn
October 3–October 30	Ruis/Elder

I have many reasons for choosing the Samhain calendar. It is my belief that the Samhain calendar is more in line with ancient time-keeping. The date of Samhain, October 31, was the ending of the old Celtic New Year and was traditionally observed as a descent into darkness for meditation and self-reflection. I also think the Samhain calendar is aligned with the Goddess's descent into death in her crone aspect, which we honor at this time of the year. The Goddess's key concept is the ending in the beginning and the beginning in the ending. In my mind, all things begin in the dark, whether it is a seed deep in the earth, an idea or plan conjured from the creative unconscious, or a child growing in the womb.

Samhain ends and begins the lunar calendar and was the primary winter ceremony in the British Isles, just as Beltane was the primary summer ceremony that falls opposite Samhain in the Wheel of the Year. Beltane is an Anglicized form of *Bealtaine*, which means May. This springtime celebration falls in the Duir/Oak month of this system and corresponds to the astrological sign of Taurus. Beltane, Taurus, and May are opposite Samhain, Scorpio, and November. In this system, placing the beginning of the year in November flows with the arrangement of Duir/Oak in May. (In the other calendar, Duir/Oak is placed in the month of June.)

Further, Fearn/Alder (which represents December 27–January 23 in this system) is inseparable from the mythological Bran, the Celtic Saturn/Cronos, who presides over January, Capricorn, and this third month of the Samhain calendar. (The other calendar puts Fearn/Alder under the sign of Aries in late March and early April.)

And there is also no debate that the sequence of the letters, trees, and months in this system corresponds to the traditional placements of the letter on the joint of each finger as I described earlier.

I find it most useful to consistently use sundown on October 31 as the beginning of the Celtic New Year. It neatly marks the end of the cycle of the thirteen moon months and a day, and I prefer the feeling of the year beginning with the final harvest and the darkening after the equinox. It seems appropriate to me to begin in the dark as we honor the Mysteries and establish a new year out of the germinating seeds of consciousness that are intentionally planted, nurtured, and cultivated.

The Other Moon Calendar

The dates are different if you choose to follow the moon calendar that begins with Beith/Birch on December 24. This calendar does not correspond to the order of the first five ogham of the tree alphabet. Nuin is moved to the third tree position and Fearn and Saille are moved down. Thus, the order is Beith, Luis, Nuin, Fearn, and Saille. This calendar is also made up of thirteen trees, not fifteen.

This alphabet order is usually attributed to the work of Robert Graves and his book *The White Goddess*, written in 1948. You can find more about this dating system online. The dates are as follows:

DATES	TREE(S)
December 24–January 20	Beith/Birch
January 21–February 17	Luis/Rowan
February 18–March 17	Nuin/Ash
March 18–April 14	Fearn/Alder

Dates	Tree(s)
April 15–May 12	Saille/Willow
May 13–June 9	Huathe/Hawthorn
June 10–July 7	Duir/Oak
July 8–August 4	Tinne/Holly
August 5–September 1	Coll/Hazel
September 2–September 29	Muin/Vine
September 30–October 27	Gort/Ivy
October 28–November 24	Ngetal/Reed
November 25–December 22	Ruis/Elder
December 23	Nameless Day/Mistletoe

Other Systems

My friend John Willmott lives a few miles from Ballinafad, County Sligo in Ireland. His friends nicknamed him the Woodland Bard, so he has adopted that nickname. John is a storyteller and performer of nature folklore and tradition from what is now Ireland, Scotland, Wales, and England. This knowledge was passed to him by his family and also through the storytellers he has visited and worked with for more than sixty years. He focuses on nature folklore because "there are many tellers of mythical battles, but too few tellers of the wisdoms of nature."

I was lucky to meet John and visit him at Carrowcrory Cottage when I was in Ireland in 2019. John now presents a weekly broadcast of "nature folklore" every Sunday via Facebook, YouTube, and Twitter.[5] Each year, five of these broadcasts are on Ogham themes.

Within one of these Ogham sessions, John presented a basic introduction to the Ogham and to the early medieval language studies of Damian McManus. McManus wrote a book in 1991 (which unfortunately is now out of print) titled *A Guide to Ogam*. McManus applied his vast knowledge of early Irish languages to medieval scribes' translations of the meaning of the Ogham symbols and their tree correspondences. He discovered what appeared to be errors in their translations from oral to scribed language. McManus concluded that some of the scribe translations did not fit the trees and shrubs they presented. When McManus researched further, he found himself creating an alternative twenty-tree Ogham set that was actually twenty native trees with no shrubs. They also formed a seasonal sequence throughout the calendar year. The forfeda were not addressed in this Ogham.

Although the actual origins are still unknown, some folklore validates coupling these four aicmes with the season of the year, each with five ogham symbols. It is also interesting to note that some folklore tells of the Ogham being memorized as musical notes. (Five notes in a scale is a pentatonic scale.) It is worth considering how many of the ancient call-and-response chants are a pentatonic scale. Thus, it is evident that music was important in the memorization of this folklore, these traditions, and the meanings and teachings of the Ogham.

Here are some of the adjustments that McManus made in his own research. Bear in mind that his interpretation is based on his profound knowledge of early Irish languages:

- Spring: Birch, Rowan, Alder, Willow, and Ash (replaced by Cherry) rule the period from Imbolc to Beltane.

---

5. More information about John can be found at www.naturefolklore.com.

- Summer: Hawthorn, Oak, Holly, Hazel, and Apple rule the period from Beltane to Lughnassad.
- Fall: Vine (replaced by the Buckthorn), Ivy (replaced by the Furze/Gorse), Reed (replaced by the Broom), Blackthorn, and Elder rule the period from Lughnassad to Samhain.
- Winter: Pine, Gorse (replaced by Ash), Heather (replaced by Elm), Poplar and Aspen, and the Yew rule Samhain to Imbolc.

And, if you are not connecting with the idea of using a Celtic tree calendar or identifying the trees with the seasons, rest assured that many do not associate the trees with a date at all! If you so choose, you can simply follow the tree teachings on your own schedule.

The Celtic alphabet is flexible, and there are many different alphabets. A perfect example of this is that some versions of the Celtic alphabet include other trees than the ones I use. I learned the Ogham system and the tree correspondences from the work of Liz and Colin Murray, who wrote *The Celtic Tree Oracle: A System of Divination*, and later I applied the trees and correspondences to the Samhain calendar. The Murrays do not place the Ogham within a time frame. In Danu Forest's book *Celtic Tree Magic: Ogham Lore and Druid Mysteries*, she also does not place the Ogham or the tree correspondences within a time frame. Her trees correspond with the ogham that I use, with some substitutions, shown in the following chart. Her differences show up mainly in the forfeda:

Samhain Correspondences	Forest's Correspondences
11. M/Muin/Vine	11. M/Muin/Blackberry
13. Ng/Ngetal/Reed/Straif	13. Ng/Ngetal/Broom/Fern
21. Ea/Koad/the Grove (shears)	21. Ea/Ebadh/White Poplar (shears)

Samhain Correspondences	Forest's Correspondences
22. Oi/Oir/Spindle (helmet)	22. Oi/Oir/Spindle (helmet)
23. Ui/Uilleand/Honeysuckle (bones)	23. Ui/Uileann/Honeysuckle (hook)
24. Io/Ph/Phagos/Beech (hook)	24. Io/Iphin/Gooseberry (bones)
25. Ae/Mor/the Sea (shirt)	25. Ae/Eamhancholl/Witch Hazel/Wych Elm (shirt)
	26. Ph/Phagos/Beech (shirt)

In Sandra Kynes's book, *Whisper from the Woods: The Lore & Magic of Trees*, the system that she describes is the same as the one I follow, except for the forfeda:

Samhain Correspondences	Kynes's Correspondences
21. Ea/Koad/the Grove (shears)	21. Ea/Eabhadh, Ebad/Honeysuckle, Aspen (shears)
22. Oi/Oir/Spindle (helmet)	22. Oi/Oir, Or/Spindle, Ivy (helmet)
23. Ui/Uilleand/Honeysuckle (bones)	23. Ui/Uilleann, Uilen, Uileand/ Honeysuckle, Beech (hook)
24. Io/Ph/Phagos/Beech (hook)	24. Io/Ifin, Iphin/Gooseberry, Beech (bones)
25. Ae/Mor/the Sea (shirt)	25. Ae/Amhanchool, Eamhanchool/ Witch Hazel, Pine (shirt)

Another author I have found is Diana Beresford-Kroeger. In her book *To Speak for the Trees: My Life's Journey from Ancient Celtic Wisdom to a Healing Vison of the Forest*, she writes from her Irish background and her knowledge of the alphabet and the trees. She presents the trees alphabetically:

- A / Ailm / Pine
- B / Beith / Birch
- C / Coll / Hazel
- D / Dair / Oak
- E / Eabha / Aspen
- F / Fearn / Alder
- G / Gort / Ivy
- H / Huath / Hawthorn
- I / Iur / Yew
- L / Luis / Rowan
- M / Muin / Blackberry
- N / Nion / Ash
- Ng / Brobh / Rush
- O / Aiteann / Gorse
- Q / Ull / Apple
- R / Ruis / Elder
- S / Saili / Willow
- T / Tinne / Holly
- U / Ur / Heather
- Z / Straif / Blackthorn

Note the difference in the names of the ogham and in the spellings. She includes only the feada. There are many systems that only address the twenty original ogham.

Creating Your Own Path

In summary, there is no knowing how correct any of these systems are. This is why no one can claim that they follow the "true" Ogham or calendar. Perhaps as more early manuscripts are translated, we will find out more information. As I stated before, this does not mean that the body of knowledge that we have available to us today is inaccurate; it is a powerful and meaningful way to create a spiritual practice and develop a world view that honors stewardship and respect for the earth. The Ogham and calendar are born out of Celtic traditions, folklore, legends, and spiritual perspective; derived from inscriptions and early manuscripts; and passed down through the generations by word of mouth,

My point is to not get too hung up on which is the "real" calendar or alphabet, or which system has the "correct" correspondences or the "correct" dates. We don't have enough information to claim that one is more real than the other. We do not know the true origins of the information that we use today, so work with the system that is best for you. You can use both calendar systems, if you'd like. In my opinion, neither is more accurate or correct. This is especially fun if you choose a birth tree, because then you can have two!

Find the system that you most align with and that brings you closest to the tree teachings. Or make up your own calendar based on your own local trees. You also don't have to use a calendar or equate the Ogham teachings to time. What I am suggesting is to follow your intuition. Be flexible with this. There is no "right" way!

What is most important is the teachings of the trees. This information is so organic and life-affirming. The trees' wisdom teaches us to be aware of the incredible gift of nature and the earthly paradise that we have been blessed with. This allows us to recognize our own sacred worth and our place within the grand scheme of life.

The Last Ten Ogham and the Wheel of the Year

In this book, I make suggestions for times of the year that you may choose to perform a ceremony dedicated to one of these last ten ogham. The aicme ailim are usually referred to as the seasonal trees, so I arrange their ceremonies within that context. I also suggest times to address the forfeda, and these are my own invention. I choose the timing of these ceremonies and their tree correspondences to loosely align with the eight holidays of the Wheel of the Year because doing so provides me with a solid structure for teaching the tree wisdom, and it helps me and my students to remember the teachings. I notice that as my students practice over the years, they become stronger in their knowledge, and they collect experiences with the unseen world that confirm their belief in miracles, magic, and wonder. They know when to honor a tree because of the timing of the year; this becomes second nature after a while. In other words, placing these last ten ogham within a time sequence allows me and my students to move through a yearly practice that is relatively easy to follow.

For me, the European Wheel of the Year is the foundation of my practice and moves me and my students through the cyclical change of the seasons. It helps us stay close to nature and to notice the seasonal changes within our environment. The Wheel of the Year's celebrations were especially important to ancient peoples, who depended on these seasonal markers to dictate when to plow, sow, harvest, and rest. These seasonal festivals have been adopted by many and interpreted in a variety of ways. The turning of the wheel represents the continuing birth, death, and rebirth of nature and life. It represents one year of life and all the years that make up one life. It is the passing of time while we are here on Earth. It represents the stages of our lives as well: birth, youth, adult, and elder. It is our responsibility, according to the teachings of the trees, to garner understanding and wisdom as we move through these cycles and practice stewardship, forgiveness, compassion, and discernment. It asks us to hold all life as sacred and to never take any of this bounty for granted, nor to misuse, dishonor, or disrespect this paradise that we exist in.

There are four lunar holidays, known as fire or cross-quarter celebrations, and four solar holidays within the modern Pagan Celtic Wheel of the Year. The Celtic year ends with Samhain on October 31 and the Celtic New Year begins the next day, on November 1. This is referred to as the end in the beginning, and the beginning in the end. Thus, there never is an ending, just a continuation, and they are really one celebration.

As we move through the wheel and encounter the teachings of each tree, we also work with the energies of the gods and goddesses and their totems. These are central to the themes of death and rebirth. The ancient people of the British Isles all honored the Goddess in her many forms and names, and she is embedded in their stories and mythology.

The Goddess represents the feminine initiations throughout life, the lunar cycles, and Gaia's seasonal changes. The Goddess has many forms, including maiden, mother, and crone. The mother goddess of summer's abundance retreats in winter to join the crone in the underworld, emerges as the maiden in the spring, and becomes the mother again by the returning summer, only to retreat in the fall. It is the Goddess that blesses and participates in the cycle of death and rebirth as she joins with the masculine, empowers the mystery, and ensures the regeneration of life through the seasons. She is the creator and the Great Mother, and thus is central to the cosmology.

The Trees Around the Wheel of the Year

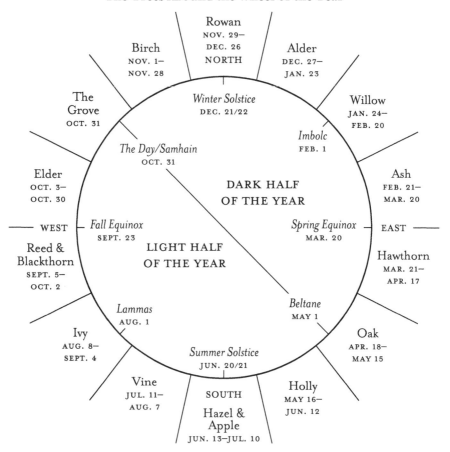

As you continue your studies, there are many maiden, mother, and crone goddesses from different areas of the British Isles that you can familiarize yourself with. There are many Irish, Welsh, Cornish, British, and Scottish goddesses. In Ireland the goddess was Domnu, Danu, Anu, Ana, Banba, Eriu, Fotla, Babh, Kessair, Kersair, Kele, Artha, Brigit, Grainme, Macha, Morrigu, and Sheila na Gig. In Wales she was Blodeuwedd, Arianrhod, Mona, Rhiannon, Gwenhwyfer, and Kerridwen. In Scotland she was the Cailleach, Bera, Brigit, Cale,

Carline, Scota, and Mag Moullach. In England she was the White Lady, Ana, Dana, Amma, Annis, Artha, Alba, Graine, Ker, Madron, Modron, Mab, Morg-Ana, the Great Queen Rigantona (later Epona), Guinevere, Vivienne, the Lady of the Lake, Elaine, and Nimue.[6] There are also many Irish, Welsh, Cornish, British, and Scottish gods to learn about. For example, in Britain the masculine is represented by the Green Man, the white stag, Herne the Hunter, and the great Horned God, Cernunnos. Lugh, Manannán, Lir, and Goibniu are a few of the Irish gods. I suggest making a list of these gods and goddesses for your own enjoyment. I keep a pile of note cards dedicated to these gods and goddesses handy so that I can do a quick review, and I'm always adding more as I continue my studies.

As you move around the wheel, I have made some suggestions for when the last ten ogham of the alphabet can be celebrated. Please check the dates of the solstices and equinoxes each year because they can fluctuate. (In my book *Celtic Tree Rituals,* you can find ceremonies for the eight holidays at the end of the tree month that they fall in.)

Each of the last ten ogham has wonderful teachings available for you, and you will form relationships with new plants, trees, and elements that will only expand your spiritual journey. You will also become familiar with the Wheel of the Year as it turns.

Dates of the Wheel of the Year for the Last Ten Ogham

Note: October 31 and November 1 are considered one celebration in the Celtic Wheel of the Year. October 31 is the ending of the year and November 1 is the beginning.

---

6. Jones, *Ancient British Goddess,* 7.

The Holidays

October 31	Samhain: Halloween, Hallowmas, All Hallows' Eve, Nos Galan Gaef / Falls within the Grove/The Day. Represents the final harvest before the long winter. It's a time to honor ancestors and embrace the darker half of the year. This also marks the beginning of the New Year in many traditions. The end and the beginning. **The Koad/Grove** ceremony, which honors The Day, can be done on or near October 31. It is not the same as Samhain; they are two different celebrations, although they can be combined if you can only do one celebration on October 31. The eve of October 30 or November 1 are good choices if you are planning a separate Samhain celebration for October 31.
November 1	The Celtic New Year: Day of the Dead, Calan Gaeaf / Falls within the Birch month. New beginnings.
December 21	Winter Solstice: Yule, Midwinter, Alban Arthuan / Falls within the Rowan month. The shortest day of the year. The days will become longer, and we celebrate the return/rebirth of the sun. **Ioho/Yew** ceremony can be done pre–Winter Solstice or on the Winter Solstice.
January 1	New Year's Day. **Ailim/Silver Fir or Pine** ceremony can be done on New Year's Day or post–Winter Solstice.
February 1	Imbolc: Imbolg, Brigantia, Brigid's Day, Candlemas / Falls within the Willow month. Marks the midpoint between winter and spring. Imbolc is a festival of fire and light, and in many Pagan traditions, celebrates the Celtic hearth goddess, Brigid. **The Oir/Spindle** ceremony can be around the time of Imbolc.
March 21	Spring Equinox: Ostara, Easter, Eostre, Vernal Equinox, Alban Eiler / Falls within the Hawthorn month. The hours of day and night are equal, and light is overtaking darkness. This is a celebration of the returning of the sun and the promise of new life. **The Ohn/Gorse** ceremony can be done around the Spring Equinox.

May 1	Beltane: Beltain, May Day / Falls within the Oak month. This marks the time of the beginning of summer in ancient days. Beltane is a spring celebration that honors the fertility of the earth. A time of lust, passion, fire, and abundance. **The Uilleand/Honeysuckle** ceremony can be done around the time of Beltane.
June 21	Summer Solstice: Midsummer, Litha, Alban Heruin / Falls within the Hazel and Apple month. The longest day of the year. It's a celebration of light's triumph over darkness and the bountiful beauty that light brings. **The Ur/Heather and Mistletoe** ceremony can be done around the Summer Solstice.
August 1	Lammas: Lughnassad, Lughnasadh, Festival of the Bread, Lughnasa / Falls within the Vine month. The beginning of autumn. This is the first harvest festival, when plants drop their seeds to ensure future crops. **The Phagos/Beech** ceremony can be done around the time of Lammas.
September 21	Fall Equinox: Mabon, the Harvest, Alban Elved / Falls within the Reed and Blackthorn month. The days and nights are once again equal, with the night continuing to grow longer. This is a time of thanksgiving that celebrates the second harvest. **The Eadha/White Poplar or Aspen** ceremony can be done around the Fall Equinox.
Summer or Fall	Because Mor honors the Great Mother and Mother Earth, I think summer is a great time to do a ceremony for **Mor/Sea**. Because Mor honors the ancestors, fall is also a wonderful time to do a Mor ceremony.

If you do not want to approach these last ten ogham by a seasonal association, you can study them and do their ceremonies by theme. Here are some of the offerings:

- **Ailim:** Looking at the bigger picture. Seeking solace and guidance from the Great Mother.
- **Ohn:** To share abundance and illumination. To create sweetness as a community. To cultivate an atmosphere of light and cooperation. To open the door between the worlds. To receive inspiration.
- **Ur:** To give gratitude for abundance. Healing. To walk between the worlds and receive regeneration.
- **Eadha:** To seek support for dealing with adversity. To seek advice and courage when dealing with challenges.
- **Ioho:** Death and rebirth. To make time for reflection and solitude. To pay attention to the soul. To contemplate death. To enter meditation and quietude in order to listen to that still voice within. To honor loss and grief.
- **Koad:** To reconnect with one's spiritual path. To sit in silence. To connect with the ancestors. To enter the sacred space of the grove. To set aside one day for spiritual reconnection and contemplation.
- **Oir:** To experience delight, joy, and a lightness of being. To receive encouragement. To receive illumination. To weave a new story.
- **Uilleand:** To seek the light and return to our true nature. To connect to true purpose.
- **Phagos:** To connect to wisdom. To learn how to read objects. To seek guidance—especially now, because of the difficulties we are experiencing on Earth.

• **Mor:** To honor the element of water, maternal lineages, or ancestry. To prepare for a trip or spiritual pilgrimage. To honor the Great Mother and Mother Earth.

Now that we have covered the basics of the Ogham, I will spend some time discussing how to honor the trees. I recommend honoring the trees in ceremony. I have included ceremonies for the last ten ogham in this book, but I will also teach you how to create your own.

How to Create a Tree Ceremony

If you are inclined to create your own tree ceremonies, I offer you this blueprint and encourage you to create on your own. I believe that this is one way to draw the tree dryads closer to you and to become better friends, developing trust as you go along.

Purpose

Determine what the themes of your ceremony will be and what you hope to impart to your participants.

Preparation

Create an altar at the center of wherever your participants will sit when you hold your ceremony. (If the work is done alone, you can prepare your altar where you usually set up items for ceremonial work.) I lay a tablecloth on a low, round table that my participants can sit around, but any shape of table will do. I choose a central candle and one smaller candle to light at each of the directions. It is good to know where the directions are in your space before you begin. I always begin calling the directions in the east as I light the smaller candles. After the east, south, west, and the north, I light the central candle. When I open the circle at the end of the ceremony, I thank each direction and release its energy, beginning at the north, west, south, east, then center. I then blow out the candles with the help of my participants.

I set up my altar with leaves, cones, and branches of the tree(s) or plant that I am working with. I also set pictures of that particular tree/plant on the altar. I collect small objects and figurines of the appropriate gods, goddesses, and totems and set them on the altar. If I have any shells, seeds, feathers, or personal items that I want to fill with the loving essence of the ceremony, I place them on the altar as well. Fresh flowers are always a nice touch. I also place examples of the Ogham itself on the altar; I have a set of carved ogham on oak fews, and I select the appropriate one for each ceremony. You can make your own set, or you can buy a set from the internet. Sometimes I make a large drawing of the ogham I am working with; I like to have my participants draw the ogham in their journal so they can become accustomed to this alphabet.

Welcome and Greetings

Welcome your participants to your ceremony and thank them for taking the time to join you in sacred ritual. Begin with greetings and introductions and state the purpose of the ceremony. Pass the talking stick and have each person say their name and why they came to the circle. Take a moment for silence and have your participants close their eyes and breathe together. Ask them to leave their daily concerns behind as they enter sacred space.

THE TALKING STICK

Choose a special stick to use in your ceremonies. You can decorate it with shells and colored ribbon if you so desire. Alternately, gather a stick of the tree that you will be honoring in each ceremony.

Share the rules of the talking stick. The holder of the stick has the floor for however the participant needs it to express themselves. There is no cross talk while someone is holding the stick. If someone needs clarification or has a comment to add, they must ask the holder of the stick if they may do so. (There is no need for the speaker to say yes to this; the speaker can respond with "No, not at this time.") There is an agreement that no one talks about another's story outside of the circle without permission. All agree to hold the circle as sacred and private.

Call the Directions

Call the directions and invite the guides, totem, deities of the tree, and the tree dryads. This sets up protection for circle work and makes your circle a sacred space. When you are done calling in the directions, stand together. Visualize a forest of trees. Tone together as you feel the power of the grove.

Here is an example that you might use for calling in the directions. Simply read it out loud. After you are comfortable with calling the directions, you can write up your own or wing it.

> "I call the east, the rising sun, and springtime. I call new beginnings and new ideas. I call the Winged Ones. I call a higher perspective to all our endeavors. I call the element of air and I honor the four winds. I honor intelligence, inspiration, and communication. I honor the trees of the east and their deities, totems, guides, and guardians.
>
> "I call the south, the midday sun, and summer. I call fertility, creativity, passion, and activity. I honor our children and our own innocence. I call the plants, flowers, and trees. I call the element of fire and honor our passions, sexuality, and desires. I honor purpose and will, action and creative endeavor. I honor the trees of the south and their deities, totems, guides, and guardians.

"I call the west, the setting sun, and autumn. I call the dreamtime and inner reflection. I call all water creatures. I call the element of water and I honor all the waters of the earth. I honor our tears, emotions, and feelings. I honor flow and receptivity. I honor the trees of the west and their deities, totems, guide, and guardians.

"I call the north, the midnight sun, and winter. I call the wisdom of the ancestors and the knowledge of our lineages. I call the element of earth, and I honor our bodies that house our spirits. I honor the rocks, minerals, crystals, gems, mountains, valleys, prairies, fields, and deserts. I honor two-legged and four-legged animals and all the creepy crawlers. I honor the trees of the north and their deities, totems, guides, and guardians.

"I call above. I call the star nations, higher dimensions of consciousness and love. I call the gods, goddesses, and the angelic realm that participate 100 percent in love and protection for all. Welcome to our circle.

"I call below. I call Mother Earth and give great gratitude for all she does to sustain our lives. I give great gratitude for all creatures and the unseen domain that nourishes us. Without her permission, there would be no flora or fauna to sustain us. She is a paradise, and it is a privilege to walk upon her.

"I call within. I honor our heart's altar, and I feed the flame of love. From this inner place we receive everything we need to know. This is the home of our own inner world tree and our knowledge and love. The heart is the true master organ, where our true eyes and ears live. This is our master message center that connects us to all that is: past, present, and future. This is the place outside time and space, and the emptiness within which all potential and possibility rest. And so it is!"

Teachings

Teach about the meaning of the tree month you are working with. You can find more about this in my books *The Healing Power of Trees* and *Celtic Tree Rituals*. There is also a lot of information on the internet. Your intention is always to open to the portal of the tree to receive its teaching and guidance. State the intention for the celebration. Examples could be inspiration, healing, connecting with the ancestors, or giving gratitude.

Sing

In appendix A, I have mentioned songs that will fit well into the ceremony themes. You can research them either by title, by author, or by album name. I provide suggestions for music, but please use whatever songs you prefer that are appropriate and connected to the theme. I suggest that you download a few of the albums listed in the appendix so that you can make your own list of songs. You can also go to the internet for women's circle songs or Pagan songs. I also recommend recordings from these performers: Jennifer Berezan, Susan Osborn, Jami Sieber, Holly Near, Cris Williamson, Libby Roderick, Charlie Murphy, Rhiannon, and Ferron.

Once you are familiar with some songs, make copies for your participants. Pass out papers with song lyrics. Introduce the drum as the connection to the Mother Earth; she is the heartbeat of Mother Earth. Practice drumming together and teach the songs, or download and play the songs if you are too shy to sing. Music is always a wonderful addition to ceremony.

Chant

I have written chants that you may use, or you may create your own. The chants included are meant to be read out loud by the leader. These can be repeated many times to build up the energy.

Guided Meditation

Take a journey. You may create your own guided journey or use the sample journeys I have included in this book. Always set the mood by asking your participants to close their eyes and go within. Allow them some time to pay attention to their breath and to let go of their daily concerns. Allow them time to be with the silence before you lead them through the journey.

Ask each participant to set up protections for traveling (more about this below). Ask them to invite in their personal totems, guides, deities, and angels to protect them and help them as they move into their astral body and travel through the portal to other dimensions. Then read the meditation provided out loud. When they return from their meditation, have them thank their helpers as you close the portal. It is important to set up protections as you open doors into other realms and to close them with gratitude when you return. At the end of their journey, allow participants time to come back, ground, and center before moving on to sharing. The unconscious can use the imaginal realm to provide information, guidance, and healing. Thus, what is offered spontaneously within a guided journey can provide amazing results.

JOURNEYING WHILE MEDITATING

When you open portals to other dimensions, I ask that you do this responsibly. It is a mistake to believe that being unable to see something means it is not real. Always invite in your personal helpers (totems, guides, deities, and angels) to protect you when you travel in your astral body during a guided or personal meditation. They will help you move into your light body, will assist with navigating as you move about in other realms, and will help you return to your body safely.

I ask that you set up your protections prior to journeying. If you are a newbie and are not aware of your personal helpers, ask the

Great Mother to assist you. She is pure, unconditional love and magic and she will not fail you. And as you work with the Ogham, you will discover your own relationships with particular tree spirits and their totems, guides, and deities that will assist and protect you.

Keep in mind that when you journey, you are opening a door. When you return, you want to close it with love and gratitude. While working with the tree teachings and their totems, guides, and deities I have only experienced growth, love, and support. I want that to be the same for you. I have found this work provides encouragement and comfort. I am not interested in negative influences that divert my attention or increase fear, chaos, or harm. I want you to invite in helpers that are 100 percent in your corner, because there are spirits that are not loving, kind, and beneficial.

We know from stories and legends that there are magical beings and gods and goddesses of death, destruction, chaos, and war. There are times to ask for their help. For instance, the Morrígan was helpful to the great warriors of yesteryear. She is a great queen that is available to warriors that must meet battle. She is fierce, as would be expected. If I were going into battle, I would ask for her support. Her energy is alive and well in another dimension. The Morrígan's presence helps us understand that we do not know everything about reality.

As you do this work, you will come to understand that there are other dimensions where spirits reside. I invite you to stay with the light. Always ask for protection from your guides and totem helpers, who are 100 percent there for you. When journeying, we enter with light and love in our hearts and our minds, and we are full of gratitude. Our purpose in traveling to other realms is to seek support, insight, guidance, and healing. The Celts have taught us that working with the unseen realms in this way is our birthright and is meant to be a positive addition to our lives.

My point is that you can connect to these realms with the purpose of receiving teaching, healing, and guidance for yourself, someone else, your community, or even a situation in the world. When you have intention and permission, you are protected with the help of your spirit guides. I encourage you to ask for permission to enter a portal. When you enter a portal and make contact, it is important that you are reverent yet strong. Portals are often found in nature in places such as caves, natural springs and wells, aged tree trunks, ancient sites like stone circles and tombs, and, of course, the imaginal door at the center of your heart.

The mysteries are not all good and not all bad. Likewise, the spirits that inhabit the other worlds are not all good and not all bad. But they are powerful, and it is important to protect yourself and to call upon your guides.

You never have to continue a conversation that is over your head or that you feel uncomfortable with. It is wise to withdraw and close the portal if you feel out of your league. It takes a long time to learn how to wield spiritual power, and it is vital to understand your responsibility with it. If you remain humble, pursue your study, and use your power responsibly, you can enter these unseen realms for healing and to create a beautiful and beneficial life. In order to be respected, you must be respectful; face your fears, and acknowledge your gifts as well as your weaknesses.

Never use your power to enter another person's space, mind, heart, or soul without permission. If you have permission to do so in order to help someone, do you work and then make sure to end the connection. I do this by clapping my hands or washing my hands. If I still feel like I have not completely disconnected from the person that I worked with, I go to a tree and ask for its assistance. If I feel that the tree agrees to help, I place my hands on its trunk and ask it to take the energy and move it down into the earth to be used in a positive way. Most large trees have no problem with this.

Remember that you can teach and share and heal, but it is not your responsibility to fix someone or to alter another's situation. You can point the way, but it is that person's responsibility to do the work. When healing does occur, it is with the permission and help of your intent and your spiritual helpers, as well as the intent and spiritual helpers of your client. It is cocreated with the help of the Divine. Gratitude is appropriate.

Investigation into the Celtic mysteries is not for the faint of heart. Trust in love, care, nurturance, and goodwill. Ask for the support and aid of ancestors, totems, guides, and deities, as well the higher light and love of the Divine. This can serve as powerful protection. This is the heart of Celtic mysticism and the resounding support of nature.

A PROTECTIVE CHANT

When you begin meditating:

> *I call in my spirit helpers—totems, guides, and deities—as I*
> *travel in my light body.*
> *I call in the love of the Great Mother Goddess.*
> *I call in the tree spirit of* (name of tree you are working with).
> *I ask that I may enter this portal to learn and to heal.*
> *I ask for your permission to travel in this way.*
> *I ask for protection and for love and light.*

When you return:

> *I give my gratitude.*
> *I promise to use the love and light that I have received for healing.*
> *With reverence and respect,*
> *I ask that this portal now be closed.*
> *And so it is.*

Sharing

Make time for your participants to share. Giving them time to write their experiences in their journals helps them to remember better. Journeys are like dreams; the details can fade quickly.

Activities

During this time, you might plant seeds, draw, or write in a journal. Choose something that grounds the teachings.

Ending

End with gratitude for the tree dryads and all the spirit helpers. Release the directions by saying, "We release the center, the above and below, the north, the west, the south, and the east with our gratitude. Thank you for blessing our ceremony. We ask that this portal be closed. The circle is now open."

Using this structure, I have created dozens of tree ceremonies. You can use this structure to create your own, or you can do something totally different. Listen to your intuition.

AiLiM–SiLVER FiR/PiNE

Ogham: Ailim (al'yem), A: ┼

Keywords: Foresight, higher perspectives, wisdom, clear sight, higher vision, higher consciousness, progress, insight, breakthroughs, help from above, regeneration and resurrection, higher levels of love and understanding

Totems: Eagle, owl

Guides and Deities: The three aspects of the Goddess; higher beings of light; angels; Mother goddesses: Danu (Irish); Dôn (Welsh), Madron, Graine, Ker (British), the Great Mother

Season: Winter, post–Winter Solstice

Practical Guidance: Look at your situation from a higher perspective. When you connect to your heart, what advice comes from your higher self?

Information: The Ogham symbol for the Ailim/Silver Fir or Pine represents the vowel sound A, "ahhh." The Silver Fir and the Pine are often interchangeable because of their similar qualities and appearances. These trees promote clearheadedness, and they offer us insight as we seek to overcome difficulty and move beyond the situations that we

feel stuck in. We are offered inspiration and release. Energy is provided to help us achieve breakthroughs and move forward.

In my work I assign this tree to the period just after the Winter Solstice, which is on or around December 21. Winter's darkness and long nights allow time for reflection and contemplation. The desire for clarity and looking at things from a different point of view go well with a New Year's celebration and the new solar cycle. This is the sun's New Year, when people often reevaluate their lives and make New Year's resolutions. It is still winter in the Northern Hemisphere, but light is returning and people are hopeful. This is a wonderful time to take stock of where you are in your life, where you have been, and where you hope to go.

These trees represent foresight and a higher perspective. The deity for the Silver Fir or Pine is the Great Mother and her three aspects of maiden, mother, and crone. She offers us signals, messages, and gifts if we take the time to communicate with her. These may come as synchronicities, dreams, visions, or people, places, and things that bless you.

These trees can be helpful anytime you need guidance and are struggling to make a decision. It is time to take a long look at where you are in your life. Honor the energies of the Silver Fir or Pine as they help you reevaluate. Seek divine clarity and guidance. You can then move toward a better future that is cocreated with Spirit. Look at your situation from a higher perspective. When you connect to your heart, what advice comes from your higher self?

When you seek the answer to a question or concern, these trees offer their guidance. Metaphorically climb the tallest Silver Fir or Pine on the mountain and become the eagle. Here you can look at everything from a different perspective, and your own personal worries and concerns may seem small compared to the larger picture. Take the high road here and address your life with a longer sight and a higher stance. Rise above things in order to seek a higher understanding. Spend some time in silence as you seek clarity. Put your hand on your heart and seek divine assistance.

Perhaps you are unable to see the forest for the trees and you need some guidance. You may be so immersed in the details of the situation or problem that you cannot move toward any clarity. Take time away from your challenges to gain perspective. Be still and become silent. Wait with gratitude.

Seek the advice of a sage person in your life. Look to your dreams as well as synchronicities for guidance. Spend time looking at mistakes made and resolve to learn from these mistakes. Put any arrogance or denial aside and be willing to dismantle any misplaced ego. Choose humility.

When you need holding, feel alone, or are separated from your loved ones, call in the energy of the Silver Fir or Pine. Invoke the presence of the Goddess. She will provide you with the mothering you are missing. Imagine the clarifying energy of these trees and the unconditional love of the Goddess surrounding you and cleansing you of loneliness, replacing that energy with hope and light. Be kind to your low mood. Treat it like a beloved child. Remember, when you are experiencing a low mood, this is not the ideal time to evaluate your life. Rather, wait until this depressed point of view clears. This will pass.

Ailim/Silver Fir or Pine Ceremony

Timing for the Ceremony
January 1, New Year's Day

Purpose
We honor the period after the Winter Solstice. This is a great time to officially celebrate the New Year and honor the Silver Fir and Pine

energies. We seek a higher perspective and guidance from Source and representatives of the Great Mother.

Preparation

Take time to be with your altar and to clean it and prepare it for a new year of revelation. This is a good day to do solo work. Bring in Silver Fir or Pine branches, needles, and cones that you may find. Be sure to ask the trees before you take them. You can usually find them around the base of the tree; there is no need to cut branches down. Also prepare a picture or representations of the ogham Ailim/A.

Have your participants bring a new journal or prepare a booklet for each person. If you make booklets for your participants, they should have a cover page and then ten blank pages. Title each blank page. Title page 1 "New Year's Resolutions." Then title the following pages in this order: Contact the Oracle; Signals, Synchronicities, Messages, and Gifts; My Accomplishments; What I Need to Complete; Letting Go; Altar Work; Meditation; Prayers and Gratitude; and My Goals for the New Year. More detail can be found in the Activity section of this ceremony.

Welcome and Greetings

Welcome the energy of the Silver Fir and the Pine. Introduce yourself and go around the circle, having each participant share their name and why they came to the circle. Then have them close their eyes and share a moment of silence to prepare for the ceremony.

Call the Directions

Call the directions and invoke the energies of the Silver Fir and Pine (foresight, higher vision) and the totems, guides, and deities (eagle, owl, the Great Mother Goddess, all aspects of the Goddess, light beings, and angels). Invite in the wisdom of each participant's higher self.

Sing

Sing songs of your choice. Use your drum and rattle. This calls in the energies and enlivens the group.

Teachings

January 1 is always a day for celebration and inviting in the new solar year. It is also a time for reflection and atonement, as well as evaluation. Here is another opportunity to let go of what was created and begin a new story for the year ahead.

The Silver Fir and Pine are trees that can see over great distances. They offer clarity and progress. You are encouraged to stop and take in the bigger picture of your situation. Take some time out from your busy life and "climb" above the situation. From this perspective, you can get a clear vision of what is beyond and what is yet to come.

Seek clearheadedness and a calm viewpoint. Take time out for contemplation before you act. Listen to your intuition and commune with Spirit for guidance. Become present in the moment. Be aware of your surroundings physically, psychologically, and energetically. Here is your power and your protection. These trees encourage stillness as you look for more information.

Chant

> What is the teaching of the Fir and Pine? Pause for reflection.
> These trees offer us guidance and direction from a higher perspective.
> Behold! We seek advice from elevated consciousness.
> From here we can step into a new year with clarity.
> We honor this higher call to evaluate our lives.
> What is the teaching of the Fir and Pine? Clear vision and loving guidance.

Guided Meditation

Ask each participant to invite in their personal totems, guides, deities, and angels to protect them and help them as they move into their astral body and travel through the portal to other dimensions. (If you are working solo, it is important to set up protections as you open doors into other realms and to close them with gratitude when you return.) Remind your group to be responsible. If they do not like something that is happening in the meditation, they can return to their bodies at any time and close the portal with their intention.

Close your eyes and place your attention on your breath. Consciously slow your breath down. Let go of the day's activities and concerns. Let them dissolve as you breathe them out with intention. Bring yourself to this room and this moment. Allow your busy mind to rest with each new breath. Focus on your heart and feed it with love.

Imagine yourself on a high mountain. Above you are many tall trees that extend high into the sky. Go ahead and trek up the steep incline to a tree that you feel called to. It may be a Pine or a Fir. Take a moment to enjoy the view as you look down on the forest and valley below. Pull the crisp air on this elevated mountainside into your lungs. The sky above is blue, the sun is shining, and the air is cool and refreshing. You hear the screech of an eagle. You look up and your eyes find it as it soars across the sky.

You begin to climb the tree. It is easy to get to the top. Take your time and enjoy the climb… When you reach the top, sit on a sturdy branch that magically supports you, just like it does the mighty eagle that often comes here to take in the view. Look out over the terrain and enjoy this perspective…

As you sit with this tree, you can look down over the valley and see your past quite clearly. It is lovely to look at the successes and what you might call failures or regrets without judgment. As you sit in the clarifying air, take a look at the *now* of your life. What are you doing? What are you about? Take some time to appreciate your situation from this higher perspective.

Perhaps it is time to make different choices. This tree offers you clarity and an infusion of spiritual understanding and courage. Your tree encourages you to take the high road and look at the big picture. Do you want to create a beautiful life? Your tree offers you unconditional love and encouragement so that you can make choices that will help you create that beautiful life. Take a moment to really feel that support and breathe it in. Breathe out what holds you back and creates fear and reluctance. You may notice the Great Mother, angels, and other beings of light as you work with these trees. Give them your gratitude and know that they are all here for you, supporting you in creating a wonderful life.

Now consider the future. There are many choices ahead for you. Which ones are the most attractive? Imagine yourself having made a future choice that you love. Invite your future self to share its wisdom with you. What does it require of you as you make new choices and resolutions? What will move you toward the future that pleases you and feels fulfilling and joyful? Allow that future choice to speak with you...

When your visioning is complete, give your gratitude to your tree, knowing that you can return to this place anytime you want to. Climb down and begin the descent from the mountain.

Come back to this room and this time. When you return from the meditation, thank the Great Mother, your guides and helpers, the Pine and Fir, and your higher self. Close the portal with your intention.

Sharing

Record your experiences in your journal or have the group share their experiences.

Sing

Choose songs that celebrate the New Year or the return of the sun. I suggest "We Are One with the Infinite Sun, Forever and Ever and Ever" (traditional chant).

Activity: Beginning a New Year's Resolution Journal

This is a time for New Year's resolutions. You can ask your participants to bring a new journal for this work, or you can present everyone with a small booklet that you have prepared. If your participants are bringing their own journals, you might make a copy of the next few pages for them to use as a guide so they will know how to label the pages of their journal and what goes on each page. You will be going through this with them, but sometimes it is helpful to have a reference.

Begin with the first page and discuss resolutions. Give participants time to begin to fill out their booklets. Go through all ten pages with participants and give them time to at least begin each page. If they don't finish filling out the booklet during the ceremony, they can write in more information when they get home.

1. New Year's Resolutions: Write down a list of your New Year's resolutions.

2. Contact the Oracle: I always use this day to consult an oracle, whether it is the tarot, the runes, or the I Ching. Have each participant draw a tarot card and think about the card's message.

If you prefer, oracle cards work just as well. Write down your findings.

3. Signals, Synchronicities, Messages, and Gifts: I seek a higher perspective as I dream into the next year of my life. I look for signals, messages, and gifts. What messages are coming from your environment and from synchronicities around you? Write these down as they show up.

4. My Accomplishments: Make a list of your accomplishments. Give yourself a pat on the back for completing what you started!

5. What I Need to Complete: List what is incomplete that you still want to finish.

6. Letting Go: What can you let go of? Are you willing to go through your house and let go of clothing or things that you have not used? Can you commit to taking a trip to a local donation center? Could you plan a giveaway at your next circle or celebration? What emotions, relationships, habits, and unhealthy beliefs are you willing to let go of?

7. Altar Work: Record how you decorate your altar for the new year. Bring in branches of Silver Fir or Pine. This represents the ogham of Ailim and the vowel A, representing foresight and higher vision. Place new items on your altar that remind you of new themes that came up for you with astrology, tarot, I Ching, or other divination methods. Carve an ogham of the Ailim on a piece of Fir or Pine, or make a drawing or painting of the Ailim ogham and place it on your altar.

8. Meditation: Sit quietly and think back to the guided meditation. What guidance was provided from your higher self? Look for messages, signals, and gifts. Record your meditation experience here.

9. Prayers and Gratitude: Write down new prayers for the upcoming year. Also take time to write down what you are grateful for.

10. My Goals for the New Year: Write down a list of new ideas and goals for the year ahead.

Ending

Read your prayers out loud and give gratitude for all your blessings. Thank the dryad spirits of the Silver Fir and the Pine for their generosity. Ask for guidance and for light as you begin a whole new cycle. Ask that the portal be closed and release the directions.

A Silver Fir/Pine Story: Gratitude and Making Plans

The beginning of a new year is always exciting. When we follow the solar calendar, we embrace activity, action, movement, decision, and intention at the beginning of the new year. I love the idea of taking some reflective time to see things from a higher perspective, like the eagle sitting on the tallest Silver Fir or Pine. There is a beautiful blue spruce right by my house, and from time to time I see a bird perch on the very top. I imagine that I am the bird and that I can see the meaning of my life from this view. Of course, every day there is something new to see. I have many tall trees in my neighborhood in Seattle. I imagine that they have been here for hundreds of years, and they inspire me to seek the advice and council of my higher self.

When I think about my life and where I have been, I am reminded of the tree's trunk and the circles within it that indicate its growth patterns over the years of its life. We can see each year in each ring and how these are reflected in the growth of the tree. Like the tree, every year of my life has had an impact upon my growth and my evolution. Everything has led to the now. I am grateful. Some years were full and joyful, and others were lean and painful. Some years I flew, others I faltered. The seasons of my life are reflected in the person I am now, and the person I am still becoming.

So much has changed in my lifetime, and so much change is ahead for all of us. I am grateful that so much pain has dropped away due to my own personal changes. I had no idea that I had so much power and so much potential. Joining with Spirit has allowed me to grow in ways that make me so much happier. I am content most of the time, and when I am not, I have the power to shift things via my own perspective. I always have a choice about how I decide to see things. I have learned to be kind to myself when I am upset or in a low mood.

It is also true that when I am bogged down with worry and troubles, there is no way I can see the forest for the trees. I have to pause my busy life and take a few moments to look at the big picture. Focusing on what is trying to happen for me is a much more pleasant experience than dwelling on the bumps along the road. When I am in a fog or downward spiral, I stop to notice my thoughts. I may not turn my negative thoughts into positive thoughts all of the time, but I can at least get them to be neutral. Thoughts drive our emotions, so it is a lot like weeding. Pull those suckers out and plant some better thoughts. Or at least open a window and let in some fresh air!

And I remind you that you are never alone. You have a guardian angel, your loved ones on the other side, your ancestors, and your guides and totems. Although most people cannot see them, they are present. If you close your eyes, you can feel that they are nearby. If you can't feel them, you can imagine them. They will come when you invite them in. They are here for your highest good, for your health, and for your work in the world. They are protective, and they often give strong warnings when we are about to make a really bad choice or are in some sort of danger. Pay attention to their guidance.

When I am down, the tree's tall presence inspires me. I am reminded that I am not alone; I am supported by higher dimensions of love, healing, and potential if I move my consciousness in that direction and ask for help. There is guidance, inspiration, clarity, and renewal. There is always the promise of resurrection. That is the great mystery that we entered when we came into this magical world. Like the shamans of old, we can build a relationship with a Pine tree or a Fir and connect to its lofty perspective and feel its great love. We can ask it for cleansing and protection as we seek to create a beautiful life by letting go of patterns that are harmful, ignorant, or disrespectful of our true nature. We open to inspiration.

These trees can also help us move forward and create out of our hearts and minds. The New Year is a great time to focus on some goals that really matter to you. It is good to give yourself the whole solar year to work on your project and to really commit to it. Why wait? Why not trust that Spirit wants to work through you? Is it time to take that trip, write that book, or meet up with a long-lost friend? I would have never gone to Egypt if I had not met my fears head on. I had to stop saying "I will never get there." As soon as I said "I *will* get there," everything changed. We are all magicians, so to speak, and our words are powerful.

Take a few moments to think about your goals for the next year and write them down. Place them on your bulletin board or write them on index cards and tape them to your mirror. Believe them. Trust that your goals will manifest. Cut out pictures of your guides and the deities that support you. Draw a tall Silver Fir or a Pine tree. Collect pine cones and add them to your altar. Work with the sigil for this ogham; write it, draw it, or carve it. Remind yourself of the magic that is around you. We are amazing beings with powers that we are just waking up to. So, like the new calendar year, let's wake up to a new year of life that is purposeful. Make today a new beginning. Focus on what you want and let the rest go. Give gratitude for what you have now and for all that is to come.

OHꞐ~GOR8E

Ogham: Ohn (on, uhn), O: ╫

Keywords: Collecting what you need to manifest your goals, sweetness, hope, persistence, abundance and generosity, magic and mystery, fertility, inspiration

Totems: Bee, magpie

Guides and Deities: The spring maiden goddesses, such as Brigid, Blodeuwedd, Creiddylad, and Elaine; Lugh; the Fae; Merlin; Taliesin

Season: Spring

Practical Guidance: Share your abundance with others. Create a sweet life. Shine your light out into the world. Be your own brightness. Practice gratitude.

Information: The Ogham symbol for the Ohn/Gorse represents the vowel sound O and symbolizes collecting and gathering. This ogham is all about community and cooperation, sweetness, and the promise of new life. We celebrate the maiden aspect of the Goddess as well as fairies, bees, and honey. The god Lugh and the light of the sun are honored.

Gorse helps open the doors between worlds, especially when we choose to celebrate the spring or summer and her energies. She invites you to receive inspiration. We reap the benefits of what nature creates, but we don't really understand the magic and mystery behind manifestation. Taking time to contemplate the Mysteries behind creation is a worthwhile endeavor. Silence and personal retreat can encourage the process of entering into the unseen world and receiving its blessings. You are encouraged to share any illumination with your community that you may have received in your meditations and your communications with Source.

The Gorse brings in the promise of spring and the abundance of summer. The bright gold color brings in the joy of new growth and renewal. It has long thorns, unlike the broom plant, which it is often mistaken for. It is a plant that can withstand fire; fire causes its seeds to open. It is an excellent nitrogen fixer and can grow even in poor soil.

I usually assign the Gorse to the time around the Spring Equinox, which occurs on or about March 21. The Spring Equinox is a day to celebrate balance and the movement toward light. The day before the equinox is often called the Day of the Gorse. The Gorse is all about fertility, passion, ecstasy, and eroticism. It is also about the budding sexuality of youth and the budding of nature. It is a call to the regeneration of life. The Gorse is all about renewed inspiration and creativity.

The Gorse is also about sweetness. How do you create the nectar of honey in your life? Be mindful of cultivating an atmosphere of light and cooperation. Work with others to create good. This is a perfect time to give gratitude for what you do have in your life by counting your blessings. Look at what you are collecting around you. Are you too materialistic and overly consumptive? Do you hoard? Do you share with others? Do you cultivate sweetness or distress and drama? If you have a goal, collect good people around you for support. Keep to the golden yellow color of hope. Persist with faith.

In olden days, Gorse was used to remedy sadness. Use it energetically to work with hopelessness and despair. The golden flowers bring in the sunlight and offer renewed hope. Place its golden flower in a vase to remind you of all that is good. It can be helpful when you need a dose of hopefulness and bright blessings in your life. It can uplift you when you feel sad or down.

Perhaps you are hiding your light. Share yourself and share what you have. Perhaps you are isolating yourself or holding on to things, hoarding your possessions. It is time to join with your community and to use your talents in cooperation with others. Perhaps you are hanging out in negativity and forgetting to count your blessings. Where in your life are you holding back, saying no too often, or refusing to share? Where are you being stingy?

In the same way that it draws bees to its scent, color, and nectar, you can use Gorse to attract a combination of forces and possibilities. The yellow flowers attract life energy and can assist you in your growth and support as you move toward fulfilling your potential. When focusing on what you want to manifest, use Gorse to attract your intended goals. Remember that you do not have to do it all alone. Ask others for help. Create something that helps others and the Universe will support you.

When you come together with others, use Gorse energy to encourage cooperation and working together toward a goal. Just having sprigs of Gorse around can remind you of this sweet intention.

You can also use Gorse to sweep away evil influences. Make a broom of its branches and sweep away what you no longer need. You may also use it to sweep away winter as a way of welcoming spring.

The Gorse is a sanctuary shrub that protects the life that lives around it. Think of this shrub when you need holding and protection. The thorns of the Gorse are a reminder to protect what is most important to you. The thorns remind us to protect nature and to hold sacred our vulnerability and our need to be appreciated and loved. This shrub reminds us that abundance is ever-present in the natural world, and that this vitality is available to us as well.

Ohn/Gorse Ceremony

Timing for the Ceremony

Around the Spring Equinox

Purpose

We seek to share abundance and illumination, create sweetness as a community, cultivate an atmosphere of light and cooperation, open the door between the worlds, celebrate the spring or summer and the energies of the Gorse, and receive inspiration.

Preparation

Set up your center area with an altar that honors the Ohn/O ogham and the Gorse. Make sure that you have a representation of the ogham. Prepare some simple finger foods and drinks. Request that your participants bring a journal, or prepare writing materials for the participants so that they can write down their thoughts after the meditation.

Welcome and Greetings

Welcome the energy of the Gorse. Introduce yourself and go around the circle having each participant share their name and why they came to the circle. Then have them close their eyes and share a moment of silence to prepare for the ceremony.

Call the Directions

Call the directions and the energies of Gorse (hopefulness, persistence, sweetness, collecting, fertility, creativity, abundance) and the totems, guides, and deities of Gorse (maiden goddesses, the Fae, Lugh, bees and their honey, magpies).

Teachings

Tonight, we honor the Gorse and the Ohn ogham. We honor the maiden aspect of the Goddess and the balance of day and night, and we welcome in the light half of the year. The Gorse is a needle-bearing evergreen that has bright yellow flowers that bloom in March and is associated with the sun; however, there is no month in which it does not retain its bloom. This is a shrub that celebrates spring and summer and the rising of ecstatic energy. It encourages passion and lust, leading to fertility and abundance. Gorse can be invoked to support lovemaking, partnership, and the "right relationship"—a relationship founded on reciprocity, respect, and equality.

Gorse links the inner and outer worlds with fulfillment, sunlight, and abundance. It is a valuable guide on our spiritual journey. Gorse provides a link between the worlds. It is a doorway to commune with the restorative power of Source. Gorse connects us to vision, inspiration, and guidance.

Gorse can be used for freshening and clearing energy. It represents the sweetness of honey and encourages us to gather what is required to move us forward. It represents collecting what we need to accomplish our goals. Gorse encourages hope and persistence.

This plant can be invoked to stimulate creativity. Poetry, art, song, dance, and storytelling fall within this shrub's influence. Gorse is also a good boundary maker and boundary keeper. It provides protection for the wildlife that lives within its roots, tangled trunk, leaves, and flowers and will also protect children and women who seek sanctuary. It is a sanctuary.

Celebrate this time of coming together as a community. It is a time of renewal, regeneration, and new life. We are called to honor this opportunity with a new vision of creative potential and a renewed dedication to share that creativity with the world.

Sing

Choose songs that celebrate spring, the equinox, and the return of the sun. I suggest "Mother I Feel You" by Brooke Medicine Eagle.

Chant

> *What is the teaching of the Gorse? Light is returning.*
> *Our lives come from the golden rays of the sun.*
> *Behold! The Gorse shines in her golden flowers of hopefulness.*
> *She offers renewal, sweetness, enjoyment, and pleasure.*
> *She is our passion, our creativity, and our vision.*
> *What is the teaching of the Gorse? Create in joy.*

Guided Meditation

Ask each participant to invite in their personal totems, guides, deities, and angels to protect them and help them as they move into their astral body and travel through the portal to other dimensions. Remind them to be responsible. If they do not like something that is happening in the meditation, they can return to their bodies at any time and close the portal with their intention.

Close your eyes and travel to a lovely sun-filled meadow. It is springtime and the flowers are blooming. Birds sing and soft clouds move through the sky. The sun is warm, and you welcome its return. Lie on your back in the grass and let the sun's rays greet you. Listen to the sounds and smell the flowers. Allow yourself to rest in this moment…

Imagine what it would be like to live in a community of peace, love, and support. Imagine a governance that protects its people and provides opportunities for all its citizens. Imagine the power of love and forgiveness. Imagine good stewardship for the paradise that is our planet. Just allow these good thoughts to be alive in your consciousness.

Spring is the time when we plant seeds. Imagine what seeds you want to plant in your life. Imagine what seeds you would plant for your community, your town or city, your state, your country, and your planet. Think about what you can do to protect the water, the earth, and the air. Think of something you can do to further the growth of your soul. Give this some time as we wait in the silence...

As you dream into this spring day, allow yourself to dream about what you would love to create. Don't censor this—just allow it to be. As you do this, you might also find yourself coming up with ideas about what you need to help you pursue and manifest that dream...

You notice a Gorse bush with bright golden flowers close to where you lie. You get up and move to the bush. As you take in her beauty, you are filled with hopefulness and a sense of prosperity. You see the bees gathering their nectar and you smell the fragrant blossoms. You too can create beauty, bounty, and sweetness. It is meant to be shared. Whether it is a song, a painting, a pie, or a visit, there are endless ways to share your gifts. Feel the courage that it may take to share what is yours to share with the world. Think about what you want to share out of your own abundance...

Give your gratitude to the return of the sun and the promise of new life. Thank the Gorse for its hopeful message.

Come back to the present time and be sure to ground and center. When you return from the meditation, thank your helpers and close the portal with your intention.

Sharing

Record your experiences in your journal or have the group share their experiences.

Activity: Focusing on Hopes and Dreams

Have each participant think about what they want to create and what they need to gather to fulfill and manifest this creative pursuit. Supply writing material so they can write down their thoughts. Give them enough time to fully address their ideas.

Then have each participant share, stating what they need as the group witnesses their hopes and wishes.

Activity: Celebrating and Cultivating Community

Pass around food and drink to honor the community that has been created. Brainstorm activities that the group might participate in to help others while sharing their light and abundance.

Sing

Choose songs that honor the maiden aspect of the Goddess or the beginning of spring. I suggest "Blood of the Ancients" by Ellen Klaver or "We All Come from the Goddess" by Moving Breath.

Ending

Offer energy to each member to encourage them to gather what they need to begin whatever they want to create. Give gratitude. Ask that the portal be closed. Release the directions and open the circle.

A Gorse Story: Cultivating Hope

For me, the Ohn/Gorse represents the hopefulness that comes to me at the time of the Spring Equinox and the return of the sun. I am eager for spring, for more light, and for a new season of growth, and that is what the equinox promises. It lets me know that winter is over. The days grow longer and are filled with more light as we embrace the promise of summer and abundance. The Spring Equinox is a good time to take a long, deep breath. Exhale the darkness of winter. It is the beginning of a new cycle of planting, a time of balance and equanimity.

The blooms of the Gorse are a bright yellow or gold color, and this reminds me of the glory of the sun. The blooms represent hope. I believe the best way to cultivate this hope is to practice gratitude. When the flowers and fruits begin to bloom in the spring and we are blessed with the fulfillment of the abundance of summer, it is hard to deny the magic of the natural world around us and its breathtaking beauty. It is a time to be mindful of the work of the fairies, devas, and dryads in the unseen realm who take care of the growing green world. It is a time that encourages our gratitude.

I can't emphasize enough how important gratitude is. We all like to be thanked and appreciated. Nature is not any different. Take a moment to close your eyes and give her a blast of your love…

Take a moment right now to write down what you are grateful for in your life. Here is my list for today: my family, my love of writing, the blue jay that just jumped on the roof outside my window, books, my love of studying new things, my sweet cat, the pink blossoms of the huge dogwood tree below my window, the light, self-forgiveness, laughter, friends, clean air and water, clouds, blue sky… My list seems like it could go on forever. You might choose to write in a gratitude journal or write something every day that you are grateful for.

Gorse represents the promise of renewal. She likes to stand alone so that she can draw the sun into her being without obstruction and then share the energy of the sun with you. If you close your eyes, you will see her standing in the sunlight, collecting the returning rays of the glorious sun. You see the bees around her collecting her nectar to make honey. Take a moment to see yourself as this beautiful little shrub and breathe in the glory and healing of the sun. Take your time with this. Allow it to penetrate every cell of your being.

Know that you can utilize this regenerating energy to create. Allow the fire energy of the sun to enter you and restore you.

There is no month in which the Gorse does not retain her bloom, and she is persistent in her growth. She encourages you to be ever blooming and to share your abundance and your gifts with the world. She asks you to shine. We all have to start somewhere, and we usually are afraid. When I first began to teach and give talks, I suffered from stage fright. But the message became more important than my fear. I found that although I began haltingly and was extremely nervous, I gained courage as I went along. After a while, public speaking became easier. Even the most accomplished person you know had to begin from a place of not knowing how to do whatever they were focusing on. I am here to remind you to share your gifts and your knowledge. Don't let your fear stop you. Think of yourself as the bright, golden Gorse. Don't let failure stop you. If you run into challenges, just get back on the horse. You might just be the light that changes someone's life. Your light can change the world.

The Gorse links the inner and the outer worlds with the promise of fulfillment and joy. Source promises us renewal and restoration. Gorse is a portal for communicating with the unseen realms and Source. Sit with the Gorse in your mind's eye and meditate. In the silence, feel your way to the messages that will restore you to balance. There you are with the Gorse and Source. Address this loving energy in whatever way is comfortable for you: God, Goddess, All That Is, Great Spirit, Universal Intelligence, Nature. The point of this communication is to experience love, grace, and ease. Enjoy yourself. There is nothing to do; simply receive and give your gratitude.

We all contend with times when we are unhappy and unfulfilled. Yet we can learn to appreciate our low times, slow times, and down times. They are important too. We cannot push to be joyful when we are not. Loving yourself through the dark times, the lonely times, and the challenging times allows for kindness and patience with the process. I like to think of these darker feelings as my dear children who require more love and attention. I find that they settle down after they feel heard and attended to.

The Gorse is here to bring you hope so that you can withstand hopelessness or despair. Allow her bright gold to saturate you with hope and faith. She will help you attract a combination of positive forces and possibilities into your life right here, right now. She is here to assist you in your growth and to support you as you move toward your potential.

Take a moment to think about what you can create that is sweet like honey. The Gorse shares the message of cooperation, trust, and harmony. She encourages you to begin a whole new cycle of creation. What is it that you want to create? Perhaps it is just a sense of peace and appreciation as you work in your garden or prepare a fresh salad. Perhaps it is the enjoyment of picking fruit and making a pie, reading a book in the sun, or taking a swim in the lake. This doesn't have to be a complicated endeavor. Spring and summer are times to really enjoy your life and the small things can bring great pleasure. Practice being in the moment and enjoying yourself.

As you think about your goals and aspirations, think about what it is that you must collect to bring them into manifestation. Do you need support, love, and encouragement, or do you need actual physical help in some way? Begin to ask for what you need and to collect what will help you. Write your goals and aspirations down and invite the golden color of the Gorse to flow into the page. Or, better yet, choose golden paper to write on! Leave it close by so that you can remember it.

The Gorse asks you to meet in community. This is how you both give and receive. Create your own grove, so to speak, and support each other. Sing, dance, and drum. And as you go through the Wheel of the

Year, give your gratitude. Do ceremony and ritual together. If you do not have a community at this time, you can still do this work solo.

Life is indeed precious, and this is a most joyful time of year. Return to your youth and embrace your inner child. Return to innocence. Breathe in this renewing energy. The soul is ageless, after all. Be playful. Enjoy springtime and any new beginnings that you have in mind. Pray for support and you shall have it. Remember that it is your own sweetness that has the power to attract good things. The Gorse is here to remind you of all the lovely possibilities. She only asks that we remember to share our abundance with a spirit of generosity, just as she models for us. The fulfillment of summer is promised, but it means little if it is not shared with others.

UR–HEATHER AND MISTLETOE

Ogham: Ur (oor), U (W could be substituted in Old Irish): ≣

Keywords: Healing, spiritual development, summer, evergreen, abundance, passion, generosity, fertility

Heather: Gateway linking the earth and the spirit world, pregnancy, fulfillment

Mistletoe: All Heal, the panacea for health and healing, represents the invisible life essence

Totem: Bee

Guides and Deities: The Fae; the mother aspect of the Goddess; Arianrhod; the Green Man; Pan (Greek); Irish healer god Dian Cécht; shamans; healers; wise medicine helpers

Season: Summer

Practical Guidance: Open to love, dreams, passion, and healing.

Information: The Ogham symbol for the Ur/Heather and Mistletoe represents the vowel U. It symbolizes spiritual development, closer

contact with the spirit world, and healing. Heather is a lovely plant with purple or pink flowers on a long stem. It blooms in the spring, summer, and fall and indicates abundance. I assign this plant to the time around the Summer Solstice. We celebrate the bounty of summer and are encouraged to share our abundance. We can walk between the worlds and receive regeneration. Heather promises creativity and progeny. Heather embodies gratitude, thanksgiving, love, dreams, passion, and healing.

Heather represents the manifestation of wishes, protection, and good luck. This plant represents a link between our earthly plane and the spirit world. Heather asks you to take some quiet time for communication with the unseen realm and Source because it can result in regeneration and healing. Healing comes to you through divine intervention. Pay attention to dreams, visions, and synchronicities. Prayer or meditation is helpful here, as is ritual. Spend some time in nature.

Perhaps you are blocking messages and are closed to help from other dimensions, be it guides, helpers, totems, ancestors, or divinity. This is a time to open up to love, dreams, and possibilities. Perhaps you feel that you are in a hopeless situation and that you are on your own. This is simply not true. Summer is a time of fullness, although you may feel that you are not in the flow. Don't beat yourself up if you feel disconnected. Gratitude for what you *do* have can get you back into a sense of connection. Also, accepting where you are in the moment is essential. Be kind to yourself. Perhaps this is a time to mother yourself with love and appreciation.

Gather Heather to manifest wishes. Place the stalks in a vase and see yourself already manifesting your desires. Feel it and know it. Place some Heather under your pillow to stimulate your dreams. Heather twigs were popular for making brooms for energetic use as well as actual cleaning. Make a charm using Heather, as it is both protective and brings good luck.

Mistletoe represents male potency, the Green Man, and Pan. In-voke its energy when you are trying to conceive—be it a child or a project. The male energy initiates things. When you seek balance for your male and female attributes, call in the energy of Mistletoe. Make a charm of it to bring good luck. Use it for rituals of change and transformation. Mistletoe is activating.

Mistletoe also represents healing and the life force that flows within us. This plant was especially sacred to the Druids and was celebrated in combination with the potency of the oak. Oak and Mistletoe were often used together to celebrate the Winter Solstice. Together, they represented invisible life essence. Other names for Mistletoe are Bird-lime, All Heal, and Golden Bough. Bunches of Mistletoe were hung as all-purpose protection. Please note that Mistletoe berries are poisonous, so they should not be consumed. The berries were often used in love incenses.

Although these two plants often correspond with the Summer Solstice, they can be helpful to you anytime you require healing. Their healing properties can be called upon energetically whenever you need.

Ur/Heather and Mistletoe Ceremony

Timing for the Ceremony

Around the Summer Solstice

Purpose

To celebrate the fullness of summer and to acknowledge our abundance. Healing. Honoring fertility. Pregnancy. (What do you want to become pregnant with?) Fulfillment. To share gratitude and appreciation.

Preparation

Set up your center area with an altar that honors the Ur/U ogham and the Heather and Mistletoe. Make sure that you have a physical representation of the ogham.

Welcome and Greetings

Welcome the energy of the Heather and Mistletoe. Introduce yourself and go around the circle, having each participant share their name and why they came to the circle. Then have them close their eyes and share a moment of silence to prepare for the ceremony.

Call the Directions

Call the directions and the energies of Heather and Mistletoe (abundance, fertility and fecundity, pregnancy, doorway between the worlds, healing, honoring the sacred) and their totems, guides, and deities (mother goddesses, fairies, healer gods and goddesses).

Teachings

Heather and Mistletoe remind us to enjoy our life and make time to celebrate our abundance with our families and communities. There is joy and gratitude for the life that is ever new. The abundance of the plant world that feeds us and the renewal of animal and human life through the seasons is celebrated. These plants are all about fertility and bounty. Fulfillment and pregnancy are promised.

Heather opens the door to the Mysteries. She facilitates communication between the seen and the unseen realms. She encourages your soul growth and spiritual understanding. She offers creativity and creation. She offers renewal and regeneration.

Mistletoe suggests pregnancy, progeny, offspring, and fulfillment. What are you pregnant with? What do you want to birth? The mystery of life and death is revisited. Mistletoe brings in healing.

Chant

> What are the teachings of Heather and Mistletoe? Gratitude.
> These plants offer us magic and mystery.
> Behold! We seek healing and renewal.
> We join with our friends and family to celebrate our abundance.
> We honor our creativity and seek spiritual understanding.
> What are the teachings of Heather and Mistletoe? The promise
> of life.

Sing

Choose songs that celebrate summer, the fullness of the sun, abundance, and gratitude. I suggest "We All Come from the Goddess" by Moving Breath.

Sharing

Go around the circle and share what you are grateful for.

Sing

Choose songs that celebrate summer and the mother aspect of the Goddess—songs of thanksgiving and gratitude.

Guided Meditation

Ask each participant to invite in their personal totems, guides, deities, and angels to protect them and help them as they move into their astral body and travel through the portal to other dimensions. Remind them to be responsible. If they do not like something that is happening in the meditation, they can return to their bodies at any time and close the portal with their intention.

Close your eyes and breathe slowly and deeply as we begin to journey together. Simply breathe as we become quieter and move more deeply into our own healing.

You begin to travel in your mind's eye until you find yourself at the center of a lovely grove of large oak trees. It is a warm, sunny summer afternoon. The air is full of chirping birds and buzzing bees and insects. The world is alive with the bounty of summer. You find an altar before you that is made of the remains of an old tree trunk, and upon it is a vase filled with stalks of pink, purple, and white Heather. Around the stalks are leaves and stems of Mistletoe with their little berries and flowers. You move closer to take a better look.

As you do so, you find yourself at the entrance of a grotto that is surrounded with an arch made of Mistletoe and holly. A large oak door opens, and you find yourself moving through the threshold. There is no fear here, only love and encouragement. As you enter the doorway, you find yourself standing in a room of pure white light. There is nothing here but the light, and there are no words to describe the peace and joy that you feel here…

Let the light penetrate every fiber of your being—every thought, every feeling, and every cell. Keep breathing deeply as you allow the healing offered here to penetrate your being. It is wise, and it knows what is needed. Simply allow this healing to take place. Remain here with this experience for a few moments…

When you are complete, return to the altar. While viewing the Mistletoe and the Heather, you think about what needs healing in your life. This may be physical, emotional, mental, relational, or spiritual. Seek advice from the spirits of these plant helpers and receive the help that comes to you. Be with the messages. Don't censor these ideas, suggestions, and promptings.

When you are ready, give your gratitude to Heather and Mistletoe. Come back to the present and ground and center.

When you return from the meditation, thank your helpers for their protection and guidance and close the portal with your intention.

Sharing

Go around the circle and have each participant share their experiences with the meditation and what they seek healing for.

Activity: Hands-On Healing

One participant stands up. The group extend their hands and direct healing energy to the participant through their hands for a few moments. Then everyone says, "And so it is!" Move on to the next participant, repeating this method until every participant has received healing energy from the group.

Sing

Choose ending songs. Suggested songs: "There Is a Secret One Inside" by Kabir or "We Are a Circle" by Rick Hamouris.

Ending

Give your gratitude to the teachings of the Heather and Mistletoe. Give your gratitude for the fullness and prosperity of the summer and for healing. Close the portal and release the directions.

A Heather Story: Breathing in the Fullness of Summer and the Fairies

Heather is an evergreen shrub, like the Gorse, and represents the fullness of summer. It has grayish, low, hairy stalks with broom-like branches and needlelike leaves, and it has tiny blossoms that are purple or white. I love this plant. You will see it bloom in the spring, stay through the summer, and bloom again in the fall. It carries a wonderful message about renewal. It is constantly regrowing and reblooming as the representative of the full summer sun and abundance, beauty, fertility, and growth. Heather offers you joy and exuberance and reminds you of your own potential and possibility. You too are an evergreen, which means that you are ever creative and ever fertile. You are always growing new ideas and adventures.

Heather is here to remind you that you create the beauty of your life through the thoughts, beliefs, emotions, actions, and activities that you create in the moments of your life. Every moment is a decision. Cultivate beautiful thoughts and you will have beautiful creations that bloom in your life. What you attend to grows. Be aware of what you place your attention on. Leave negative thoughts alone, and if you can't move to a positive thought, at least choose a neutral one. I know this takes discipline, especially when we are tired or discouraged or ill. Nonetheless, this is the law of how things manifest in the this dimension. Heather shares with you a powerful truth: Our thoughts have power.

Heather offers you protection and energetic cleansing, and she brings you abundance and good luck. She can help you manifest your wishes and can come to you in your dreams. I think we all need a boon of good luck and encouragement during these challenging times; we all need reassurance that everything is going to be okay.

Heather is a symbol for the Great Mother, and she offers love unconditionally for you. Feel her love, breathe in her love, and let the magic of the unseen world wash you clean. Bring the summer sun into your life right here, right now. This is real, and this vibration is at the heart of all growth. Be full now and enjoy yourself. Give your gratitude and step forward into all that you can be. There is no need for doubt as you were born to grow, expand, and evolve. It's in your nature.

Heather asks you to take some time to commune with Source—however you define divinity—to enrich your soul. Healing is offered to you in this sacred silence. She is here to remind you that behind all visible forms is in an invisible power that can be relied upon. She reminds us that the Universe is for us; the unseen power of love and oneness has our back.

Heather represents the gateway linking the earth and the spirit world. This plant reminds us to get in touch with nature and to honor Gaia, Mother Earth. This plant reminds us to open to magic, dreams, visions, and the mysteries of the growing world of the vegetation on the planet. In the world of the flora, we give gratitude for so much that occurs in the unseen arena. We give our gratitude to the elemental helpers: the devas of the plants, the fairies of the flowers, the dryads of the trees, and the guardians of the elements.

Have you ever seen a fairy? I know some people have. Alas, I have not. But I have sensed their presence. I get happy just thinking about these little creatures and the work they do within the plant kingdom. Fairy glens, home to many fairies, are gateways to the unseen realm. I had an experience with fairies that brings to mind the need to be respectful of these amazing and magical creatures.

I was taking a walk in a fairy glen in Ireland. The deeper I walked into the woods, the denser the forest became. The glen was narrow and went down into a narrow ravine. The ravine was tucked between high, impressive rock cliffs on either side that were totally eclipsed with foliage. The path was full of trees and underbrush and a little steam meandered through. I had two metal walking sticks with me, and as I walked farther, the ends of the rods began to stick in the mud. Finally, they twisted off. The handles became loose, and all the different settings for increasing or shortening the walking sticks also came loose, all at once. My walking sticks proved useless and only impeded my progress.

I became aware of a growing sense of discomfort as I tried to continue. I finally stopped and registered that the unseen presence of the fairies was communicating with me. All at once, I remembered that fairies do not like metal. They were not happy that I had brought these metal sticks into their home. *Oh*, I thought, *I need to backtrack and apologize*, which I did. I was embarrassed that I was so ignorant. I left the glen, and as soon as I walked out of the woods, my sense of discomfort left.

Fairies have their likes and dislikes, and it bodes well for us if we can be cognizant of this. Although I didn't get to enjoy the glen like I was hoping, I did learn a valuable lesson, and it was still a magical experience. I didn't have trouble with my walking sticks in any of the other places I used them. There didn't seem to be anything wrong with them; they worked fine.

You really don't know when magic will show up or what form it will take. As I walked in my neighborhood today and retold the fairy glen story to my husband, I looked down and saw a beautiful little feather stuck in the earth, standing straight up. I took that as a fairy message. I imagined the little fairies smiling as I explained the lesson I had learned.

Take a summer walk around your neighborhood and see what magic shows up for you. Notice the insects, bees, birds, trees, and the plant life. Take in the smells of this bounty. Notice the flowers and all the diversity. Feel the breeze and the sun on your face. Commit to enjoying this walk. Take your time with it. Give yourself permission to enliven all of your senses and perceptions. You may even find a Heather plant or sense a fairy…

When you get home, draw the ogham for the Heather and the Mistletoe, paint it and put it on your altar, or carve it into a wood surface you have prepared. The more you work with the Ogham, the more they will reveal their magic and mystery to you. Choose pictures of

Heather and Mistletoe to display on your altar, or draw or paint your own. The more you bring in the energy of Heather and Mistletoe, the more they will share their teachings. Their presence will become familiar to you. You are cultivating a lovely friendship of mutual affection. Also bring in pictures or representations of the fairies; there are some wonderful fairy flower books that bring feelings of delight and mirth. Attention is your payment; you may enter the world of magic through your intent. Bring gratitude, a sense of wonder, humility, and appreciation, and you are likely to be invited back.

EADHA–WHiTE POPLAR/A8PEN

Ogham: Eadha (ayda, EH-yuh), E: ≣

Keywords: Adversity, endurance, determination, spiritual strength, courage, protection and shielding, messages, small voice within, success after difficulty, movement, moving through change

Totems: Horse, white stag

Guides and Deities: The crone aspects of the Goddess; the Cailleach; the Green Man; Pan (Greek); Herne the Hunter; Cernunnos, the great Horned God

Season: Autumn

Practical Guidance: You are moving through this situation.

Information: The Ogham symbol for Eadha/White Poplar and Aspen represents the vowel E and is symbolized by meeting adversity with courage. I assign this tree to the time around the Fall Equinox as the earth prepares for winter in the Northern Hemisphere. This tree bids you to listen to the whispers of the leaves as they move in the winds that finally encourage the tree to let them go. Watch the leaves as they change color and fall to the earth. This is a time of the final

harvest and clearing the dead leftovers. It is a time for composting and returning nutrients to the earth that she will use after the winter.

The totems of Eadha are the horse and white stag. The crone aspect of the Goddess is honored. Herne the Hunter, the stag god Cernunnos, and the Green Man of the woods are our guides here. Pan oversees the green growing cycles.

Within the Celtic mysteries there is a male cycle of birth, life, sacrifice, and death or renewal. The hunter is grateful to his prey and he joins with his community in ceremony to express gratitude for the life he has taken that will sustain his people. Whether it is an animal or grown vegetation and grain, life is reaped to sustain the people. The Green Man and Pan encourage the growth of this life. The hunter, farmer, or king takes what nature provides for the good of his people, his family, and his community.

Symbolically, in taking the life of the great stag, Herne the Hunter becomes the great stag god Cernunnos. A mere human takes on the wild male potency of life. He mates with the Great Goddess for the renewal of his community and is then sacrificed at the end of the cycle. He represents the death of the stag, the end of the vegetation cycle, and his own death in defending his people as a warrior or a leader. No matter how he walks through the gate of death, there is the promise of new life. The cycle begins again. A new hunter, farmer, or king is destined to become the next one that provides for his people. Respect and gratitude are essential to this great turning.

The crone aspect of the Goddess is also a guide for the Eadha. The crone is honored here with an emphasis on endings and new beginnings. This Goddess is our midwife in death and birth. With the feminine cycle, and with these trees, we honor old age and the sharing of wisdom by the elders in our communities. This is expressed through the life cycle of infant, youth, adult, and elder. In the feminine, it is expressed in the maiden, mother, and crone, as well as the return to the otherworld. We all must return and pass through the veil. Fall honors the end of life stages and the end of our lives—at least in this dimension.

In the fall we recycle and compost what is left of the harvest. The vegetation has sacrificed itself for our lives. This is true for the animal that is hunted, the plants that have given us life, and the warrior who gives up his life to rule or to defend his people. There is a sacrificial theme here: life is given so that life can continue.

The White Poplar or the Aspen represents the death of the growing season. There is less light and less warmth. As leaves fall to the ground, they return their nutrients to the earth. They follow the sun as it moves toward the Southern Hemisphere. In the same vein, these trees offer us solace as we move into the darker times of life, times when we might lose our health, relationships, or identities. These trees represent the aging process and old age that eventually leads to our own deaths.

These trees offer us the strength to endure any adversity. White Poplars and Aspens promise success after difficulty. Troubles are like storms—they eventually end. Sometimes we just have to hunker down and wait the storm out. Afterward, when the sun comes out, we leave our place of protection to see how everything faired, to see what is left. We made it through, although there may be trees down and houses blown apart. Still, we are alive, and we can begin again.

Challenging experiences provide us with an opportunity to build our character. Difficulty and struggle help create strength and resolve. And yet, when we are going through hard times, it is hard to muster the strength to keep moving. Sometimes we are asked to surrender. There is no avoiding the reality that we all experience suffering; surrender to this with as much self-love as you can summon. In times like these, I ask that you be as kind to yourself as possible. It is not always necessary to be working on yourself. Acceptance and patience are teachers.

The energy of these trees will help you with shielding and protection, endurance and courage, and success after difficulty. These trees give us the strength to deal with adversity. When you seek advice for dealing with your challenges, you are reminded that you are moving through this situation. If you listen carefully, you will receive messages from the rustling leaves.

Perhaps you are tempted to give up and give in. You may feel that the cards are stacked against you and that there is absolutely nothing you can do to turn the tides. However, in the same sense that the White Poplar offers endurance and progress, this sense of helplessness will not last. You are encouraged to endure and persist as you move through this time of stagnation or loss. Things will indeed change. Change your sense of gloom by allowing the leaves of the White Poplar or Aspen to speak to your heart. Go out in nature and listen to the trees.

Cycles are part of the nature of life. A period of distress cannot stand forever; spring will return.

Eadha/White Poplar and Aspen Ceremony

Timing for the Ceremony
Around the Fall Equinox

Purpose

We seek assistance for dealing with adversity and cultivating endurance. We seek advice for how to face our challenges. We seek protection and shielding. We ask for courage and assurance that we will overcome difficulty. We honor the crone aspect of the Goddess as well as our crones, elders, and teachers.

Preparation

Collect one rock for each participant. Wash the rocks prior to the ceremony, as these rocks will become paperweights. Make sure you have enough black markers for each participant. Provide glue and swatches of felt as well. More information can be found in the Activity section of this ceremony.

Welcome and Greetings

Welcome the energy of the White Poplar and the Aspen. Introduce yourself and go around the circle, having each participant share their name and why they came to the circle. Then have them close their eyes and share a moment of silence to prepare for the ceremony.

Call the Directions

Call in the energy of the White Poplar and the Aspen. Call in the guides and deities. Call in the great male and female cycles of life. Call in the energies of autumn. Call in the crone, the horse, and the white stag. Call in courage and persistence to meet adversity. Call in strength and guidance.

Teachings

Share pictures of the White Poplar and Aspen. These trees offer you courage and the ability to overcome and endure your troubles. Thus, you are offered the gift of strength, perseverance, and courage. You are provided a strong shield against difficulty or misfortune. These trees offer you protection. While you may have hard work ahead of you that requires tenacity to defend yourself from an opposing force, these trees remind you of your inner strength and the resolve that you need to meet a struggle. The promise is victory, so don't give up. They also will provide you with guidance today. They offer a strong stabilizing effect and are strong healers. They help you bring balance to your life. All life is cyclical. If you are in a period of difficulty, spring will come again. There is no stopping this truth. This will pass.

Chant

> What are the teachings of the Poplar and Aspen? Inner strength and resolve.
> These trees offer us protection and courage.
> Behold! We are offered a strong shield against difficulty and misfortune.
> We are reminded that we have everything we need within ourselves.
> We can meet challenges with fortitude and tenacity.
> What are the teachings of the Poplar and Aspen? Victory.

Guided Meditation

Ask each participant to invite in their personal totems, guides, deities, and angels to protect them and help them as they move into their astral body and travel through the portal to other dimensions. Remind them to be responsible. If they do not like something that is happening in the meditation, they can return to their bodies at any time and close the portal with their intention.

Envision a tall White Poplar or Aspen tree. It is a cool autumn day and there is a stiff breeze. You notice that the leaves have already turned colors as the wind animates the branches of your tree. The air is fresh and clean, and you take a deep breath as you look up at the tree and see the thousands of leaves rustling in the wind. It is as if the tree is singing. Just listening to the sound of the leaves calms you and centers you. The song changes as the wind moves and sways the branches of the tree in different directions. Sometimes the sound is intense and other times there is a lull. Take time to simply be with this experience...

Let your tree know the difficulties you are going through and the challenges you are facing. Take your time with this. Feel the acceptance that this tree offers you. Listen to what the tree has to say...

What advice does the tree share with you?

Ask the tree if there are any final messages for you. Take a moment to listen to the ending message that the tree has for you...

What is the message?

Take a moment to send your tree a blast of love and gratitude. Send her health and acknowledgment. Know that you have received guidance from love and light and Source energy. Know that this tree is now your ally. You can return to her just by closing your eyes and seeing her in your mind's eye anytime you so desire.

Before you leave her, allow your tree to strengthen your resolve and encourage your strength and flexibility to handle what is before you... Breathe in the strength and the protection that you are offered. Give your gratitude to your tree and allow her energy to balance, protect, and encourage you.

When you feel ready, begin to return to this room and this time. Thank your helpers for their protection and guidance and close the portal with your intention.

Sharing

Pass the talking stick so participants can share their experiences. What are the challenges they shared with their tree? What advice was offered?

Activity: Creating an Eadha Paperweight

Provide clean rocks and black markers. Have participants write the ogham for Eadha on their rock. They can use it as a paperweight and a means to remember the teachings of Eadha in withstanding challenge and adversity. Have them glue a piece of felt on the bottom of the rock to protect any surface it will be used on.

When the participants have finished making their paperweights, go around the circle and have each participant hold the rock near their heart. Have them close their eyes. Then ask each participant to promise to remember these teachings when they go through a difficult time. Ask them to verbalize their promise in their own way.

Sing

Choose songs that celebrate the changing of the seasons or that honor the crone or the harvest. I suggest "We Are the Old Ones" by Flight of the Hawk or another ending song.

Sharing

Ask the participants to go around the circle and share the names of crones, elders, and teachers that they admire, as well as a little bit about them.

Ending

Stand and have each participant take turns saying a prayer for themselves, loved ones, or anyone else who is going through a challenging situation. Have them use their hands to energetically direct the prayers into the center of the circle. Give gratitude to the circle, then send the created energy out into the world to heal using your group's intentions. (Have everyone sweep energy from the center with their palms open, then raise their hands to release the energy to the sky.) Ask that the portal be closed and release the directions.

A White Poplar/Aspen Story:
Making Friends with Adversity

Years ago, my husband and I planted two Poplars in our backyard. We no longer live on that property, but it is still a special place for me. When we moved, I had no idea that I would see those Poplar trees in my mind's eye many, many times. Every once in a while, we drive past our old property just to check out the trees. Now, twenty or so years later, the Poplars have grown tall and unencumbered. I see them reaching for the sky and they remind me that I can meet any adversity.

How do we overcome adversity when it confronts us? I have been thinking about that a lot lately. Since May of 2017 I have been recovering from a terrible bout with Ciprofloxacin antibiotic toxicity. I have been "floxed," as they say. Fluoroquinolone antibiotics can have horrible side effects. Thankfully, this doesn't happen to everyone who needs this strong antibiotic. And although I spent almost a year on the couch, it has been over four years since this disaster, and I am grateful that I am mostly recovered.

You too might be suffering from a difficult situation. Perhaps it is an acute situation like mine was, or perhaps it is a chronic condition that could even be life-threatening. Your situation may be affecting you physically, emotionally, mentally, or even spiritually. Perhaps it is financial or an issue in your love life, or maybe you are experiencing intense grief after losing a loved one. I know many of you who are reading this are going through your own dark night of the soul. Whatever the nature of your difficulty, I believe that these two trees can offer solace and strength. If you invite these trees to help you, they will offer you comfort, as they did for me.

When I was sick and in pain, unable to walk or live my life, I had to face my fears. I resolved to keep my thoughts positive and clear. I kept saying, "Even though I am having symptoms, I know that my body knows how to heal." I must have repeated this sentence a million times! I remembered the teachings of the White Poplar. I refused to become a victim. I knew that there was much to learn from this situation: patience, perseverance, and faith; courage and resolve.

During my recovery process, I often thought about the two Poplar trees that my husband and I planted in the backyard of our old house. The trees just kept popping up in my mind's eye. They appeared quite stately, and I was impressed by their size and stature. Focusing on them helped me change my energy. I was refreshed simply watching these tall trees sway in the wind; I was mesmerized listening to the sound of their leaves.

I invited in the energies of the Poplar trees. They offered me courage and the ability to overcome and endure. I asked for their protection and imagined their gift of a strong shield against this misfortune. I was reminded that even though I had to be diligent with my healing regimen, they would strengthen my tenacity. It took tenacity to stick to my routine and to stay positive. Basically, my life became about detoxing and placing important nutrients back into my body that had been stripped away. This required a lot of patience and staying present in the moment. I dismissed all thoughts that painted bad scenarios in my future; I just refused to go there.

The Poplars reminded me of my own inner strength and the resolve that I needed to face my difficult situation. White Poplars promise victory, so I didn't give up. I was reminded over and over that my body knew how to heal. The heart knows how to heal as well. Healing has its own time frame; it cannot be hurried. The trees reminded me to be patient. I relied on their guidance and their stabilizing effect. Indeed, they are strong healers. I hope that you will call upon these tree helpers to sustain and strengthen yourself if you need to. They are eager to help.

Remember that the trees do love to be thanked. They love to be appreciated. When you walk by any tree, say hello and give it your gratitude. You may be surprised by what happens next!

IOHO–YEW

Ogham: Ioho (yoho, EE-yoh), I, J (Y could be substituted in Old Irish): ䷀

Keywords: Eternity, everlasting life, death and rebirth, transition, endings, letting go, reincarnation, cemeteries, ancestors, longevity, counsel and advice, strength, ancient wisdom, the otherworld, loss and grief

Totems: Raven, crow, owl, vulture, snake

Guides and Deities: The crone aspect of the Goddess; the Grim Reaper; Taliesin; death gods and goddesses; ancestors and loved ones that have passed through the veil

Season: Winter, post–Winter Solstice

Practical Guidance: Let go. Allow for change. Embrace change. Be kind to yourself. Honor your grief process. When it is time, you can begin again.

Information: The Ogham symbol for Ioho/Yew represents the vowel I and symbolizes rebirth, legacy, and the ancients. For me, this represents the time after Samhain, up to and including the Winter Solstice. Another name for the Winter Solstice is Yule. It marks the beginning of the return of the sun to the Northern Hemisphere. It is a rebirth moment. As the ancients prepared for winter, it was crucial to store up enough food to make it through. They had to adjust to the shorter days and longer nights as they kept warm by their fires and filled the evenings with songs, music, and stories passed on from their ancestors. This is how they shared their teachings and wisdom. This is a time for us to open to the dark and the quiet. Take time for reflection and cut back on activity. Sit in silence. Then celebrate the rebirth of the sun.

The Yew tree embodies death, rebirth, and reincarnation, as well as endings, transitions, and transformation. The Ioho ogham stands for letting go and beginning again. We are invited to develop our intuition and to reconnect to our ancestors and our spirituality. The guide for Ioho is the Grim Reaper, who comes for us all when it is our time to pass through the veil. The deity is the crone aspect of the Goddess. This is the dead of winter, the darkness before the light. Death. To the ancients, death was but a door to a new level of experience. When one crossed that threshold, they would be reunited with their loved ones, pets, and ancestors. And for the living, there was the promise of rebirth—the return of the sun and the spring—but they had to get through the challenges of the winter first: intense cold, hunger, and illness.

We are not faced with the same challenges today, but we all have to deal with "small deaths" in our lives. The Yew lets us know that an ending is indicated. What are you done with? What (or who) is asking you to let it go? You are invited to embrace change. You may not know where you are going, and you do not need to. Trust the process. Something is dissolving so something new can be birthed. It is necessary. You might fight the invisible by putting off a decision, or you might avoid letting go of someone out of fear. Allow this tree to walk you through the steps you must take in order to move on with your life.

This ogham deals with loss and grief. You may be dealing with the death of something or someone; grief is appropriate. But grief can be so overwhelming that it is hard to function. The Yew is here to remind you that grief is a process. Each of us has our own timeline, and we are allowed our own grieving process. Yet all of us need help from time to time, especially during times of loss. Please seek professional help if you feel you are sinking into depression. There are others who can hold you and comfort you on your dark days.

Even though loss and grief are a part of life, these are some of the most difficult emotions. Many of us have loved ones that suffer from mental illness, alcohol or drug addiction, incarceration, or poverty. We suffer loss through divorce, financial difficulty, or addiction. We may lose our home, job, possessions, or even our mental capabilities. The loss of a parent is hard; the loss of a child is harder. This can also include loss through abortion or miscarriage. Although adoption or foster care offer hope for a child, these hold their own stories of grief and loss as well. And there is loss when one desires children and is unable to have them.

My point is that loss and grief are major themes in life. Dealing with these emotions can be difficult. This may sound strange, but sometimes I think the spirit of a tree can be more comforting than another person. I don't have to worry about burdening the tree, and the tree doesn't offer words that may set me off or impede the healing process. Of course, there are humans who can be helpful too, but many people just don't know what to say or how to help. That is why I suggest working with a trained grief counselor.

I think the Yews are the oldest grief counselors on the planet. They stand as sentinels, offering their support and encouragement during every difficult situation that humans have faced throughout history. They are strong and steady, and they understand our sorrow, our sadness, our longing, and our grief. Imagine this tree in your mind's eye. The Yew can live for thousands of years. She has seen everything and can hold your sorrow. Allow the Yew to comfort you.

Perhaps you are in a period of transformation. Perhaps you are fighting this. Pushing through your feelings or holding them down with your willpower isn't relevant right now. Patience is the only way through this time. Surrender to what is. Don't fight the process of feeling your feelings. Grief seeks to be experienced, and only then will it let go of you. Seek solitude *and* seek the love and comfort of others. Seek the love and comfort of the ancestors, the spirit world, and Source. Create boundaries with folks that drain you or are unhelpful. The Yew encourages you to feel what you feel unconditionally and promises that the thaw will come. She will stand by you throughout the process.

Ioho/Yew Ceremony

Timing for the Ceremony

After Samhain, up to the Winter Solstice

Purpose

To honor our ancestors and loved ones that have passed over and to seek their guidance. To connect with the unseen realm and the Mysteries for regeneration and solace. To make time for silence, solitude, and reflection. To honor winter. To pay attention to the soul. To contemplate death. To enter mediation in order to listen to that quiet, still voice within. To honor grief and the grieving process. To honor our losses. To contemplate cycles, change, beginnings and endings, rebirth and regeneration.

Preparation

Set up your center area with an altar that honors the Ioho ogham and the Yew. Make sure to include a physical representation of the ogham.

Welcome and Greetings

Welcome the energy of the Yew. Introduce yourself and go around the circle having each participant share their name and why they came to the circle. Have them close their eyes and share a moment of silence to prepare for the ceremony.

Call the Directions

Call in the energies (endings and beginnings, death and rebirth, communication with ancestors, and the otherworld) and totems, guides, and deities (raven, owl, vulture, the Grim Reaper, gods and goddesses of death) of the Yew.

Teachings

This tree grows in such a way that it allows itself to stay in the same place for centuries. Its branches grow down into the ground to form new stems, and these form the trunks of new trees. When the central trunk becomes old and decays, a new tree will grow from the old one and continue to feed from the same roots. You will often find these trees in British cemeteries; some are known to be more than two thousand years old. The message is that no matter what is encountered in life, a new start always presents itself again. In every ending is a new beginning.

The Yew also symbolizes a connection to the ancestors and their wisdom. They have much to share with us if we invite them in. They are our best cheerleaders and are invested in good outcomes for us. They have gone through the experience of death, and they understand that this passing is but a doorway to another realm of life.

The Yew will honor our losses and support us in our grief. This tree teaches acceptance and patience.

Sing

Suggested songs are songs about winter, death and rebirth, the crone, or the ancestors. I suggest "Blood of the Ancients" by Ellen Klaver.

Chant

> *What is the teaching of the Yew? Rebirth.*
> *Our bliss comes from letting go.*
> *Behold! It is our nature to survive our grief and begin again.*
> *And we seek her comfort and solace as we heal from our losses.*
> *We honor her age and wisdom.*
> *What is the teaching of the Yew? Transformation and new*
> *beginnings.*

Guided Meditation

Ask each participant to invite in their personal totems, guides, deities, and angels to protect them and help them as they move into their astral body and travel through the portal to other dimensions. Remind them to be responsible. If they do not like something that is happening in the meditation, they can return to their bodies at any time and close the portal with their intention.

In your mind's eye, travel to a cemetery in Britain. There is a small church with a bell tower, and you see a smattering of stone grave markers through the weathered iron fence that encloses the graveyard. It is a cold day in late fall, and you draw your coat collar up around your neck to stay warm. As your eyes look out over the land, you are drawn to a huge Yew tree that stands just beyond the cemetery. You follow a path that leads to the tree so that you can commune with this ancient and wise friend.

As you take in the tree with your eyes, move closer so that you can feel the bark of the tree's trunk. It is very thick, as it has grown over and over around the original tree planted there so long ago. Then sit down with your back against the Yew.

Slow down your breath and breathe deeply. Feel the grass where you sit. Feel the strength of the tree as you lean against it. Allow your breathing to slow down as you tune in to the heartbeat of your Yew…

See if you can sense the Yew's heartbeat. As you sync your breathing to her heartbeat, you slowly begin to hear her message for you. Your tree is happy to communicate with you. If you do not see, hear, feel, or sense the message, allow yourself to imagine or simply receive. Be with the stillness and the quiet…

If you are going through a time of sorrow or grief, take a moment to share this with your tree. This may be a time to remember loved ones you have lost or perhaps to just invite in your grief. Allow your tree to comfort you. Breathe in her fragrance and her kindness.

Take a moment to think about others who are struggling. You may also remember situations that you have struggled with or are facing right now. Feel the tree offer you comfort and support. The Yew understands challenging times; feel her deep compassion and strength. Breathe in the healing and the encouragement offered to you. Stay with this for a few moments…

The tree offers you wisdom as you move through the changes that life presents to you. The Yew reminds you that you are an immortal spiritual being just visiting for a short time in an earthly body; you are on a soul journey. The tree encourages you to live responsibly and wisely. She offers you some innovative ideas that support the sacredness of your life…

Take a moment to thank your tree for her gifts. Bless your ancestors and loved ones that have passed on; they are your cheerleaders. Your ancestors and loved ones also whisper wisdom. Take a moment to hear any messages they have for you…

When you are ready, return to the present. Ground and center. Thank your helpers for their protection and guidance and close the portal with your intention.

Sharing

Have each participant share something they gleaned from their meditation. Encourage them to share the names of those they have lost. Or perhaps they would like to share their biggest loss, whatever that may be. This could also be a time to talk about failures, challenges, disappointments, and betrayals. Perhaps they are holding on to regret, resentment, guilt, or shame. Remind the group that the sacred space created in this ceremony is a healing cauldron that can hold pain and suffering and support the grief process. Take your time with this; give everyone a chance to speak their truth without judgment. Often our pain and suffering become less intense when we are able to express them and know that we are heard.

When everyone has had a chance to speak, have the group stand and hold hands around the circle. Have them close their eyes and imagine a grove of Yew trees standing around the circle, holding the circle. Tone together and allow the joined sound of the group to become one with the trees. Have your participants imagine that each one of them is an individual tree within this grove. Ask them to allow the energy of all that has been shared to move through their leaves, branches, and trunk, down into their roots and down into the earth. To the tree it was just energy, but the earth will use this energy to promote life. Give this a few moments.

When this feels complete, give gratitude to each tree and the grove, and have the participants return to their body and the circle. Have them open their eyes and look around the circle, making eye contact with each person.

Sing

Choose songs that celebrate the changing of the seasons or that honor the ancestors. I suggest "We Are the Old Ones" by Flight of the Hawk.

Activity: Experiences of Being Loved and Appreciated

In the spirit of our loved ones and ancestors being our best cheer-leaders, take a moment to remember them. They went through the challenges of life and suffered their own losses.

Have each participant think of a loved one that has passed over or an ancestor that is "in their corner." This could also be a totem, guide, or deity from the unseen world that has offered encouragement and support.

Have each participant share an experience that allowed them to know that they are loved and appreciated.

Ending

Give gratitude to the helpers and the energy of the Yew tree. Then ask that the portal be closed and release the directions.

A Yew Story: Suicide as a Teacher

Many people have had experiences with dreams, synchronicities, visions, and guided meditations that allowed them to receive healing and guidance from ancestors, loved ones and pets that have passed over, or totems, guides, and deities from the unseen realm. The spirit of the Yew invites us to ask for these communications of love, forgiveness, and regeneration. The Yew reminds us of the interrelatedness of all life and of our deep connection to the mystery of all that is. The Yew stands to connect us to this wisdom and to open us to healing. It offers spiritual water that we are thirsty for.

In May 2019, I walked in a cemetery in Ireland that held ancient Yews. The Yew trees there are thought to be over one thousand years old. As I leaned into one of the trees, it shared a message with me. I heard, "Ha! And you think *you* are old." That made me laugh. Indeed, these trees planted in cemeteries have a thing to say about watching and witnessing births and deaths, baptisms and funerals, the joys of saying hello and the grieving that comes from saying our final good-byes to our loved ones.

You will often see Yews in the cemeteries of the British Isles. They can be hundreds or even thousands of years old. They stand as senti-nels as the dead are buried. They keep watch as families and friends visit graves. One cannot think about the Yew without contemplating death and what it means to the living.

People die in different ways. My father died of cancer of the esoph-agus at eighty years old, my mom drowned at the age of sixty-five, my best friend was shot in a car hijacking at the age of forty-nine, and another dear friend died of Lou Gehrig's disease in his late thir-ties. My brother's baby boy died in the first months of his life of crib death. Some people just die in their sleep when they reach a ripe old age, like my husband's father. And then there is the story of my friend who committed suicide at the age of fifty-five.

Suicide is a difficult subject. If you or a loved one are experienc-ing mental health issues, I suggest reaching out to a professional for guidance and support. There are also suicide hotlines, which can provide valuable assistance. I wish my friend had considered these resources.

When a friend or loved one is suffering, it is challenging for every-one involved in that person's life. And when a person chooses sui-cide, it's an extremely painful process for the loved ones left behind. There is no easy way to talk about this or to relay the circumstances. My dear friend had been severely depressed and unhappy for a long time. We were shocked when we heard that she had committed suicide. It was devastating, and I will always grieve her death. I am sorry that we couldn't have helped her more.

I was elected to run her memorial service (I think because no one else wanted to do it). I had to be brave. We held her service in the same grove of trees where we had celebrated her fiftieth birthday in Seattle's Lincoln Park. She had asked me to priestess that birthday for her, so perhaps that is why her memorial service fell to me. My friend was someone who attended most of my tree ceremonies and circles, and she was a woman who loved the trees. We had walked in Lincoln Park and enjoyed the trees together countless times.

My husband, Ricardo, had a family friend who had committed suicide, and Ricardo had the experience of channeling a communication from him. In this letter, this young man explained to Ricardo why he had committed suicide. He had been severely schizophrenic and had suffered terribly from this mental disorder. Ricardo chose to share this communication at the young man's memorial service, and it seemed to help alleviate some of his loved ones' suffering.

Ricardo had a similar experience with my friend after she died. When he closed his eyes and went inside and listened closely, he received a communication from my friend that he wrote down. He chose to pass her communication on to me to read at her service.

At the ceremony we drummed and sang, which my friend loved to do. We went around the huge circle of people and everyone spoke about her. She was loved by so many. We fully celebrated the joy that this woman had brought into our lives. It seemed fitting that the full, hot sun of the summer fell upon us as we celebrated this Leo woman's life.

And then we had to talk about how she died. And of course, people were sad and upset and baffled. I read the channeled letter from her after explaining that it came through my husband. I read the letter in the hopes of relieving some of their despair. This is the letter:

Sweet Sharlyn, my loving friend,

Do you know that I love you totally? And I know you love me totally, even when you are mad at me for leaving you in the way that I did. I thought of many ways to kill myself, but this was the only way I could actually do it. I did not think of how it might affect you or those who found me. I am sorry for that. I wanted to say goodbye, but nobody would listen. They'd just try to convince me that I should not want to die, that I should want to live. I did not want to end up hospitalized or go on medication or go through all that. I really wanted to just die.

My death is not a horror. My life was a horror, and I did not know what to do about it but this. Now I know there are lots of ways. I am in a good place, except I hate seeing you suffer so. I was suffering too, and I just could no longer bear it. I could no longer bear imposing on you or others with my bitter despair. I could no longer afford to risk more frustration and disappointment by putting myself in the hands of a "professional" with expertise who could not guarantee any results.

Please don't worry about me. Don't even miss me. I am still with you. Actually, I am more with you now than when I was living my hell. I am with you in the form of those beautiful roses that came to you through that beautiful eight-year-old boy and your loving husband. Notice how they too are dying even as they bring you love and beauty. Death is not a bad or even a sad thing. It is but one aspect of the eternal cycle. Remember that Indian prayer that also came to you through your husband? I am you, sweetheart. I live in you.

All my love forever,
Your friend

My friend was talking about the following poem, which was once thought to have Native American origin. It is now thought to have been written by Mary Elizabeth Frye.

Do not stand at my grave and weep
I am not there. I do not sleep.
I am a thousand winds that blow.
I am the diamond glints on snow.
I am the sunlight on ripened grain.
I am the gentle autumn rain.
When you wake in the morning's hush
I am the swift uplifting rush
Of quiet birds in circling flight.
I am the soft stars that shine at night.
Do not stand at my grave and cry;
I am not there. I did not die.

My friend's death was one of the most emotionally challenging experiences of my life. Perhaps my husband's letter was his way of offering us understanding and acceptance. I cannot know if the letter was indeed a communication from my friend; I like to believe that it was. Celtic teaching says that is indeed possible, and that our loved ones are always close and willing to communicate with us.

As I ponder this, I conjure up the Yews in the cemetery in Ireland and ask them for some solace, some wisdom. Soft words come to me. *It is not how we die. We all die. It is a doorway. It is another adventure. Yes, miss your friend, but celebrate her.* I wish my friend was still here. I miss her so much. And I deeply wish that we could have provided her with the help that would have changed her mind. Yet, when I think of her, it is almost as if she is echoing the message from the ancient Yew trees, and I hear these words: *Please don't linger on how I died. Think about our moments together. All the laughter and tears.* That makes me smile.

KOAD~GROVE

Ogham: The Koad: ✕

Keywords: The temple, silence, initiation, recommitment to spiritual path, communicating with ancestors and loved ones who have crossed over, the star, spiritual renewal

Totems: Personal totems, owl

Guides and Deities: Personal guides and deities; the crone aspect of the Goddess; Nemetona, the goddess of the Grove; the god of the dead, Donn (Irish); Arawn (Welsh), who rules the dead as Lord of Annwn, the Welsh otherworld

Holiday: "The Day," October 31

Practical Guidance: Forgiveness will set you free. Your ancestors and the loved ones beyond the veil are your cheerleaders.

Information: In the British Isles, ancestors used to meet under the Groves. The Groves stood as the ancient people's churches and holy places. This fall day at the end of October and the beginning of November marks a time to sit in silence and get in touch with your own spiritual life and your connection to Source.[7] It is a time to reconnect with your own personal guides and guardians and offer gratitude for their help and support. It is a time to pray and devote yourself to your spiritual practice. It is a time to visit your temple, synagogue, or church or explore the great outdoors. This ogham represents the temple, the silence, the void, initiation, meditation, recommitment to the spiritual path, and communication with ancestors and loved ones who have passed on. This is a time to prepare for winter. Pay attention to the soul and enter meditation so that you can listen to that quiet, still voice within.

The Grove represents the most important celebration and holiday in the Celtic cosmology. "The Day" falls on October 31 and marks the end of the Celtic year. The celebration of Samhain, Hallowmas, All Hallows' Eve, and Halloween are also celebrated at this time. You can choose to celebrate Samhain on this day, which honors those who have passed on as well as the ancestors, or you can focus on spiritual renewal. Or do both! Whichever you choose, take some alone time to meditate.

The Koad is representative of all knowledge, initiation, the temple, the holy of holies, and the great silence. Here we work with crone and wise old wizard energy. Embrace the Mysteries. This is a day that we give gratitude for our spiritual helpers. You are invited to make space to connect with your guides and totems. The teachings of the Grove invite you to reconnect to what is spiritually meaningful to you and to give your gratitude. Take time to sit in silence and to review your year. Listen to the messages from the ancestors. Contemplate death. The Celts readily made space for the dead and believed that they sent healing, guidance, and support to the living. Connect with your ancestors and with loved ones that have crossed over the veil.

---

7. Even though the Koad is number twenty-one in the Ogham system, it represents The Day and is added to the thirteen moon months of the Celtic tree calendar to make 365 days of the year.

Stand within the protection of the Grove and enter sacred space. Focus on the essential energy of the Universe that is unnameable and unknowable.

The Grove also represents your community. Spend time with like-minded people in ritual and ceremony. It is time to reconnect with your Source. Do you have a place that is sacred to you? Do you have a spiritual group, coven, temple, Grove, or church that is meaningful to you? Do you have a spiritual practice that supports you? What spiritual lineages have meaning for you? It is time to connect to a community if you have been isolating yourself. Your isolation may be cutting you off from important regeneration.

Of course, the 2020–2021 lockdown that we experienced during the global pandemic caused us to be isolated for well over a year, but at least we built some coping strategies. And if nothing more, the lockdown made us more thankful for our support groups and our spiritual connections.

Perhaps your life before the pandemic was too busy and you had little time to go within. For many, working from home during the pandemic made life even more hectic. Stress and worry have been our daily diet. Many have found themselves at home with nothing to do, staring at their four walls. There is no denying that this necessary isolation has been painful, and most of us have sought out unhealthy habits to comfort ourselves from time to time. Perhaps you discovered that even as the world slowed down, you still had difficulty stopping and mediating or setting aside time for contemplation, prayer, ritual, or ceremony.

The fact is that we could all benefit from meditation and contemplation, especially during challenging times. We could all use a reboot after suffering increased anxiety, nervous energy, and fear. This is a good time to put our worries, fears, and concerns on the back burner. This is a good time to breathe slowly and consider the teachings of the Grove.

This ogham asks you to think about what truly sustains you, and the Grove invites you to set some boundaries and some priorities for your inner life. Have you become so overwhelmed with the outside world that you have forgotten about your inner world? Do you fill every moment with noise, drama, and activity? Have you been drinking too much or overeating? Do you spend too much time playing video games, watching television shows, or scrolling on social media? Do you ignore your own needs and put all of your energy into caring for others or working? Perhaps it is time to return the focus to yourself and your authentic needs.

I think the pandemic made many of us aware of a need for change. There is work to do. This is an excellent time to face our fears and consider the changes that we avoided. The Grove offers some questions that you might ask yourself: Have you forgotten that you are a powerful spiritual being? Have you turned a blind eye to your own hopes and desires? Have you stopped considering new possibilities and potential? Have you lost sight of your inner worth and value? Have you given way to despair? Have you forgotten that you are a part of nature? Have you forgotten how to trust? Have you asked for help? Would you allow the spirits of the Grove to assist and support you?

Take some time to reflect upon these questions while taking a time-out from your usual schedule. At first, sitting quietly without an agenda can be uncomfortable. Sitting in silence for even five minutes is a reminder that your inner life and your connection to your spiritual nature is just as important as your other activities. Your connection to spirituality is actually where your energetic fuel comes from. It is the inspiration and the renewal, allowing you to carry out your goals and responsibilities. Your spiritual connection needs care and attention. It is here in the quiet that we can receive regeneration, renewed hope, and the resurrection of faith.

Koad/Grove Ceremony

Timing for the Ceremony

The eve of October 30, October 31 (if you are not doing a Samhain ceremony), or November 1

Purpose

To reconnect with one's spiritual path. To sit in silence. To connect with the ancestors. To enter the sacred space of the Grove. To set aside time for spiritual reconnection and contemplation. To create relationships with totems and guides in the unseen realm. To seek renewal and regeneration. To listen to messages about a new cycle of life. To receive insight and inspiration from the mystery and magic of the Universe.

Preparation

Prepare your altar with the Koad ogham and pictures or symbols that represent the Grove. Have your participants bring pictures of loved ones and pets that have crossed over. They can also bring in pictures or symbols of their guides, deities, and totems.

Welcome and Greetings

Welcome the energy of the Grove. Introduce yourself and go around the circle, having each participant share their name and why they came to the circle. Have them close their eyes and share a moment of silence to prepare for the ceremony.

Call the Directions

Call in the energy of the Grove. Call in ancestors and loved ones that have crossed over. Call in your personal guides, deities, and totems. Call in the energy of the higher realms of love and understanding as well as the star nations. Call in the angels and the realms of earth, air, and sea.

Teachings

Nowadays, people often meet in spiritual communities in places like synagogues, churches, cathedrals, mosques, and temples. Our ancestors often met in caves or sacred wells, on top of mountains, and under Groves of trees. The Groves of the British Isles were sacred meeting places for ceremony, ritual, celebration, and gratitude. Groves were a sacred place, a gathering place for powerful spirits and communication with other realms of consciousness. Groves often sat upon natural springs and were enclosed or marked by trenches or fences. The goddess of the sacred Grove was named Nemetona. Gods associated with her are Loucetius (British), Llew (Welsh), and Lugh (Irish). Often, local gods and goddesses were invoked as well.

You can choose to celebrate The Day, which embraces your connection to Source, or you can celebrate Samhain, which represents an ending and a beginning. On Samhain, we remember the dead and seek communication; we give gratitude for their help, their guidance, and their protection. We remember. I like to celebrate Samhain on October 31 and The Day on either October 30 or November 1; this way I get both celebrations in.

Within the Grove, we find assistance in communicating with loved ones and ancestors that reside in the otherworld. Assistance is offered to us when we take the time to communicate with Source, totems, guides, and deities as well as the unnameable essence of universal knowledge, wisdom, light, and creation. Celebrate with a community of like-minded people.

On this day, choose to interact with the mystery. Make time to meditate in the silence. Enter the void where all is created. Within this space we find forgiveness, love, solace, and regeneration. Let go of your grievances and allow the light to replace your regrets, resentments, and old stories of pain. Release worn-out perceptions, ideals, values, and plans. Open to the new.

This is a day to give your gratitude for what has been and to thank the totems, guides, deities, and tree spirits that have informed you throughout the Celtic year. Honor the Goddess in her many forms. Honor your loved ones that have passed on.

Activity: Naming Pets and Loved Ones That Have Crossed Over

Go around the circle, having participants name people and pets that have passed on that they love, honor, and miss. Have them share any pictures that they brought with them to the circle. If they feel comfortable, they can also share about their own guides and totems—some people choose to never disclose the identities of their personal helpers.

Sing

Choose songs that have to do with the Goddess and sacred space. I suggest "Where I Sit is Holy" by Shaina Noll and Russell Walden.

Chant

> What is the teaching of the Grove? Unity.
> We are stronger together than alone.
> Behold! The Grove provides a safe haven to commune with Spirit.
> Nature is our true home.
> Here we find our ancestors and loved ones that have passed on.
> What is the teaching of the Grove? The mystery is our teacher.

Guided Meditation

Ask each participant to invite in their personal totems, guides, deities, and angels to protect them and help them as they move into their astral body and travel through the portal to other dimensions.

(If you are working solo, it is important to set up protections as you open doors into other realms and to close them with gratitude when you return.) Remind your group to be responsible. If they do not like something that is happening in the meditation, they can return to their bodies at any time and close the portal with their intention.

Close your eyes and breathe deeply. Be with your breath as you move deeper and deeper into the silence. Allow the quiet softness to envelop you as you let go of any stress, worry, or concern. Breathe deeply in the simple act of doing nothing as you enter this quietness…

You find yourself at the entrance to a grotto or cave. You do not enter, but you know that there is a lot of energy here and you feel a sense of anticipation. Soon you notice that people are beginning to come out of the cave. They are dressed in their best clothing, but from many different times in history. You see that a group of people is forming a half circle in front of you.

Those standing directly in front of you are dearly loved friends and family that have passed through the veil. You can feel them all sending you love and encouragement, so there is no fear here. Next to your parents or aunts and uncles are your grandparents, and next to them, your great-grandparents, and next to them, other relatives, and so on. The circle becomes larger and includes those who have traveled from farther back in time. You keep stepping backward to make room for the growing circle.

You feel an overwhelming sense of protection and joy. The ancestors and your loved ones are feeding you with appreciation. You are their living power and proof. You have all their dreams standing upon your shoulders and so you are their fulfillment. Give your gratitude. You carry their best hopes and aspirations, and they are delighted to support you here. Take a moment to receive their messages…

Your pets that have crossed over will probably show up as well. They are so incredibly happy to see you and interact with you. They send you a blast of love and you return it. Listen to the barks and meows and the sounds of the chirping birds. Take a moment with this…

Now new people begin to circle up in front of you. They stand within the half circle of those that have passed over. These are your loved ones that you share this incarnation with. They may be your children or any children that you love, teach, and influence. They may be your grandchildren or great-grandchildren. They could be your nieces and nephews and their children.

Now notice a new half circle forming in front of those that you love in this incarnation. It is a growing group of people coming from the future. You realize that they are your loved ones that are yet to incarnate. You have not even met them yet. You feel an overwhelming sense of love for them. Send them love and encouragement. Send them your messages. What is it that you think is essential for their well-being? What is essential for the well-being of the planet? Send this group a blast of love. Take some time with this…

As your time at the cave comes to an end, you will see your loved ones that have passed on return to the cave that leads back to the otherworld. As they leave, they let you know that they will greet you and help you when it is your turn to walk over the threshold. The animals return to the cave as well, but you feel their love. Then it is time for the loved ones of this incarnation and of the future to dissolve back into the ethers. You feel great love for them and for their aspirations and choices. You feel immense encouragement to be so connected to your own lineages. Breathe this in…

Focus on yourself for just a moment as you stand alone in front of this magic cave. Look at your life. Take stock. Are you happy with where you are and what you are doing? What would you like to accomplish or receive or manifest for your next year of life? Just be here with these thoughts as you contemplate another year's passing. Allow love to fill you and motivate you and protect you.

Just when you begin to think about returning home, you notice a light coming from deep within the cave. As you stand at the entrance, you see the light growing. It builds in intensity until two beautiful spirits show themselves to you just within the entrance. You are quite amazed to see them—and maybe even a bit frightened, especially after the visitation from your loved ones of the past, present, and future.

It appears that these two spirits are shining. One is a lovely but ancient crone—a medicine woman, a light bearer. You recognize her. She has an aura of great love and understanding. The other is an ancient wizard, a wise and withered elder, a shaman of great wisdom and knowledge. They are both dressed in long white gowns and wear wreaths of forest greenery and flowers upon their heads. She holds a scepter in one hand and a lantern in the other. He holds a staff in one hand and a lantern in the other.

She speaks and says, "Behold! We represent your higher self in male and female form. We bring light to encourage you and to guide you along your path. You are indeed a bright and beautiful child of the Universe, full of potential and creativity. We are here to remind you that you are magical. You are never alone."

Next, the wizard has something to say: "Hello, dear one. We are your inner lights. We offer you assistance and grace. Take time to listen to our messages. Take time for prayer, meditation, and quiet time. Let us know what you need and when you are lost, insecure, and frightened. Let us help you when you are confused and do not know which way to turn. Focus right behind your heart at the doorway of your inner tree. We will teach you about the Mysteries and the magnificent, and we will strengthen you when you are confronted with evil and malice. We protect you. We are your stars, here to remind you that your soul is also a shining star and that you are a light bearer for the world."

They both hold up their lanterns and the brilliant light totally overwhelms you. Close your eyes and stay there for a moment, taking in the renewing energy. It feels like megadoses of healing and love. When you are able to open your eyes, you see them both smiling at you. They nod as a way to say that it is time for them to return to the cave and to travel to their own higher realm in the sky. They reassure you that they will be ever present for you, but now it is time for them to leave. You watch them as they return to the cave, and the light diminishes until there is only darkness.

You are in awe. You give them your gratitude and love. Thank your ancestors from the past who have crossed over, your loved ones in this current incarnation that visited you, and your future loved ones. Send love to your pets that visited you.

When you are ready, return to the present. Ground and center. Thank your helpers for their protection and guidance. Close the portal with your intention.

Sharing

Have your participants share their experiences from the Grove meditation. What was it like to receive love from their loved ones and ancestors? What was it like to send love and support to their future relatives? What changes do they have to make to allow for greater expression of who they are and what they want to accomplish? What was it like to meet their own higher selves? Did they receive any messages?

Activity: Listening to Music and a Short Silent Meditation

Have your participants scttle in for a short, ten-minute meditation. Play gentle, soothing music. Harp music is nice; I recommend Peter Sterling. Ask the participants to imagine a nice grassy place to sit in the middle of a Grove of their favorite trees. Have them say prayers while in meditation—for themselves, their friends and loved ones, their coworkers, the planet. Have them give their gratitude to Source, however they name that.

Sing

Choose songs that have to do with mystery. I suggest "We All Come from the Goddess" by Moving Breath or "Song to the Mother (I Walk Your Sacred Ground)" by Danean. Choose an ending song like "Merry Meet" (traditional chant).

Ending

Give your gratitude for this special day and for the Grove. Thank the ancestors and loved ones that have passed on and the pets that you miss. Thank them for their guidance and love. Thank those who walk into the future. Make prayers for the planet and for healing. Make prayers to take care of the earth. Give your gratitude for the guidance and support of the higher realm beings of love and light. Ask that the portal be closed and release the directions.

A Grove Story: Connecting with Source

Celtic spirituality teaches that we can cross thresholds and walk through gateways to other worlds and realms via our imagination. Nature provides access to magic places and mystical lands through its sacred places. In Ireland, caves, wells and springs, the ocean, rivers and lakes, trees, and mountains are portals to the unseen realms. There are similar places in nature wherever you live; these are called "thin places," as the veil between the worlds is more permeable in these spots.

Sacred places all over the world are powerful for eliciting direct communication with higher dimensions of love and light. They hold a vibration that helps you communicate with your ancestors as well as totems, guides, and deities. In Egypt, it is the sacred sites of the temples and tombs that hold the energy to support this communication. In the British Isles, it is the stone circles and the prehistoric tombs, megaliths, and cairns. These are places where the otherworld connects to mundane reality. Ritual elements such as fire, water, trees, and stones as well as statues and relics can heighten this connection. Ceremony and ritual also provide sacred containers for working with the unseen realms.

My most memorable experience of merging with divinity came in 2012, when I led a group ceremony honoring Isis at her temple on the island of Philae in southern Egypt. It was my first time leading a group, and I was in charge of the spiritual pilgrimage for sixteen intrepid souls that had traveled to Egypt with me from the States.

My group and I traveled to the island of Philae in the dark. This was necessary to ensure that we had a private visit at the temple before tourists began arriving at 8:00 a.m. It was around 3:30 a.m. or so when we boarded a small motorboat and sped toward the island of Philae. When we were close to the island, we looked up and high above us was the temple of Isis, lit with spotlights at the bottom of the structures that left it beautifully outlined against the night sky. Our captain turned off the motor so that we could sit in the quiet water and experience the silence and the sacred presence of the temple. We could feel and hear the slight movement of the water as it gently lapped at the sides of the boat. Other than the noise of the water, we were cocooned in silence. What a beautiful moment it was.

A few minutes later, we disembarked at a dock. I led my group up the stairs and into the broad courtyard. We waited there for a bit so that my group could take in the length of the row of columns that moved us toward the entrance. Then we proceeded to walk into the smaller court through the tall pylons of the temple. There they waited while I went into the temple, walked down the long hallway in the dark, and entered the holy of holies, the inner sanctuary of Isis.

There I laid out the temple cloth and turned on the many battery-operated candles I had brought from home. Soon the sanctuary was bathed in a twinkling light. I could see the hieroglyphs and the carvings of Isis on the three adjacent walls. I signaled my group to come inside and, one by one, they walked forward. We sang "Om Tare Tuttare Ture Soha," calling in the Goddess, as they entered. Each put something of meaning upon the altar—a necklace, a stone, or an amulet.

From the time my group entered and stood around the altar until the end of the ceremony, I do not remember anything. (My friend from college who came on the trip reported that she knew that it was me leading the ceremony, but she also said, "That wasn't you!") I believe that Isis took over the ceremony by entering my body that night. It was not a feeling of violation, but a blessing. The ceremony had to do with love and forgiveness for ourselves and for others. The participants came forward to ask for healing, and I believe they received it.

As we began to close down our circle, swallows began to come in from the little windows cut high up in the rock. They sang loudly to welcome the dawn, and they flew from one side of the building, through our sanctuary, and out the windows on the other side. We were totally serenaded and surprised by their song. They seemed to celebrate with us, and I slowly began to return to my body.

It was finally time to end the ceremony and give gratitude. Our tour guide came in and said it was time to go out and greet the rising sun. As each group member left the sanctuary, they gathered their things from the altar. My husband stayed with me to clean up. We gently took the things form the altar and the altar cloth and put them in my basket. My heart was very full, and I was in a state of bliss. We sat down for a moment and I burst into tears as I grounded my experience into my body. They were tears of relief, happiness, and gratitude. Isis did visit and did bless us, and I think she took over for a while. What a lovely, unexpected blessing.

––––––––––––

The Grove can be a reminder that it is time to reconnect with Source, God, Goddess, Spirit, divinity, the Universe, and one's higher self. I am not religious, so I don't have a visual for this. I think of it more like the unifying principle of life. And a feeling…

The light and love of divinity can show up as a god or goddess. That day at the temple of Philae, the form of divinity came as Isis for me. Humans get along with symbols and we like to picture things, making them humanlike. We try to express vibration, love, and light in music, songs, art, dance, writing, or poetry. If we are quiet and receptive, Source is close. Spirit will renew. Divinity will present itself. We can have an actual experience.

I like to set aside time on The Day to meditate, play spiritual music, and give my gratitude to my ancestors, my native homeland, legends and stories, and my personal totems, guides, and deities. I also make my prayers to Source. For me, this day is a spiritual reset, a realigning of soul back to Spirit and the magic and mystery that makes up my world.

Find a place in your city or town or neighborhood that harbors a Grove of trees that you can visit. Imagine this as your cathedral. Sit quietly and reevaluate your connection to Spirit. Perhaps you require an update or refresher no matter what religion you practice. Reaffirm your own essence as a spiritual being. What brings you closer to Source? Recommit to taking time to replenish or renew that relationship. What do you need to do? Are you willing to meet your creator halfway? Reestablish your commitment to your spiritual practice. Do you remember a time in your own life when you, spontaneously or with intention, had a direct communication with the Divine?

There are many avenues to connect to the unseen realm. You can seek out this communication, yet sometimes it comes without invitation. Messages may come your way through dreams, prayers and supplications, synchronicity and serendipity, visions, daydreams, and premonitions. Movies, books, and art can spur the imaginative processes. One can astral travel in sleep or do active imagination through the inner work of journeying or meditation. Sometimes messages grab your attention through spontaneous writing, dance, bodily symptoms, or unusual and unexplainable experiences. There are a multitude of ways that Spirit contacts us. Be patient and remain open. Ask and you will receive—this is the way it works, and you will be better for it.

OiR–SPiNDLE

Ogham: Oir (or), Oi, Th: ◇

Keywords: Fulfillment, sweetness and delight, weaving, fate, destiny, thunder and lightning, sudden insight, illumination and enlightenment

Totem: Thunderbird

Guides and Deities: Lugh; Thor (Norse); thunder beings; the weaver goddesses; Brigantia (British); goddesses of fate and destiny; light beings; angels

Season: Early spring

Practical Guidance: If you don't like your life, change your thinking. Begin to weave a new tapestry. Choose light, love, sweetness, joy, and delight. It is time to stop talking and get busy. Create a new chapter.

Information: The Ogham symbol for the Oir/Spindle is the helmet. It is formed by touching the index fingers and thumbs at their tips, and it stands for the vowel combination of Oi and the consonant combination of Th. It represents fulfillment, insight, light, and lightning. It is all about sudden insight and awakening. We honor the thunder beings, the light beings, Lugh the god of light, the goddesses of spinning and weaving, and the three fates. The Spindle helps us

to experience fulfillment, sweetness, delight, joy, illumination, and a lightness of being. The Spindle encourages us to see the light in every person we meet, and in every situation. With the energy of the Spindle, we can weave a new story.

Oir can be celebrated in early spring, around the time of Imbolc, which brings the sun's light to the earth after the darkness of winter. There is a mysterious quickening within the seeds of the earth, a magical zapping that calls for the seed to grow. The Spindle is a tree that represents this sudden quickening as well as sudden insight. The god Thor is all about thunder and lightning, sudden flashes of light; Lugh is the god of thunder and lightning in the Celtic tradition.

Success is promised, but the hard work must come first. This tree invites you to put off decision-making until you get all the facts and are done with the preparatory work. Choose to do your best and be worthy and hardworking. Spindle is a good wood for making pegs, bobbins, and spindles—practical tools. Think of the work that goes into fashioning such wood implements. True sweetness comes from fulfilling your tasks at hand to the best of your ability.

Perhaps you have to wait for your fulfillment. Keep to the task at hand. Don't lose faith. Are you feeling impatient and impulsive? Better to practice patience and know that your rewards are coming through your determination and your persistence. This is a time to look within and evaluate yourself. What must be addressed and acknowledged before right action can be undertaken? Let the transformation forces do their work. You stand on a threshold. You may feel stymied, but in truth you must look at all that has brought you to this doorway, this gateway. Take your time and avoid hasty decisions that may bring you more difficulty. Your time will come. The buds of flowers bloom in the spring, and so will you. You can't force the bud to bloom before it is ready. The Spindle offers you encouragement and a jolt of light, an activation. When the time is right and all is in place, you will receive your reward for a job well done.

Oir/Spindle Ceremony

Timing for the Ceremony

Around February 1 and Imbolc

Purpose

To experience delight, joy, and a lightness of being. To receive encouragement. To receive illumination. To weave a new story. To receive a jolt of inspiration. To begin. To be activated. To keep to the task at hand. Ask for insight and illumination and you shall receive it.

Preparation

Prepare an altar space with the Oir/O ogham and pictures of the Spindle tree. Have participants bring a new blank diary with them.

Welcome and Greetings

Welcome the energy of the Spindle. Introduce yourself and go around the circle, having each participant share their name and why they came to the circle. Have them close their eyes and share a moment of silence to prepare for the ceremony.

Call the Directions

Call in the energy of the Spindle and her totems, guides, and deities. Call in illumination, sudden insight, and quickening energy. Invite in Lugh and other light beings, the weaver goddesses, and the thunder beings. Invite in the angels.

Teaching

This sturdy little tree has tiny white flowers in June and bright red, lobed fruits in the fall. We are grateful for the teachings of the Spindle. This tree is associated with women's magic and skills. She is primarily used to make spindles for weaving. Weaving is associated with fate and destiny and symbolizes domestic security and peace. In addition, weaving is always associated with the weaver goddesses. These goddesses keep women and children safe, bring abundance, and encourage creativity. The Spindle works hand in hand with these goddesses and can help us rework the threads of our own weaving when we find that what we are creating is not worthy of our love and energy.

The Spindle represents sweetness and delight. She also brings sudden insight, illumination, and enlightenment. This tree supports inner knowing and helps us complete projects and tasks. She is not interested in our evasions and excuses—she is not interested in skipping steps. She reminds us that fulfillment comes after a job well done. She supports us as we complete our obligations so that we can move forward and promises us a sense of satisfaction that will come after hard work and the application of our skills.

The Spindle is also an activator. In a bolt of lightning, the expression of light is awesome to behold. It gets our attention, never mind the thunder that accompanies the lightning strike. This sudden expression of energy is what I call a Spindle moment. It is an awakening—a sudden aha moment. This flash of understanding, of insight, or of enlightenment can activate us to do something worthwhile with the information or illumination that we received.

Sing

Choose songs that honor the spring, Brigid, or the maiden aspect of the Goddess, or choose songs that call in light. I suggest "The Dance of the Moon and Sun" by Natural Snow Buildings, "Earth Our Body" by Moving Breath, or "Oh, Great Spirit" by Adele Getty.

Chant

> *What is the teaching of the Spindle? Sudden insight.*
> *We awaken to sweetness, delight, and sudden intelligence.*
> *Behold! We seek the bright white flash of illumination.*
> *We honor the light and invite it to heal us.*
> *True delight comes from completing the tasks at hand.*
> *We choose not to evade, but to work to the best of our abilities.*
> *What is the teaching of the Spindle? Fulfillment comes from*
> *our best efforts.*

Guided Meditation

Ask each participant to invite in their personal totems, guides, deities, and angels to protect them and help them as they move into their astral body and travel through the portal to other dimensions. (If you are working solo, it is important to set up protections as you open doors into other realms and to close them with gratitude when you return.) Remind your group to be responsible. If they do not like something that is happening in the meditation, they can return to their bodies at any time and close the portal with their intention.

Close your eyes and breathe deeply as you begin your journey to the Spindle tree. You find her overlooking the ocean. Breathe in the salty air and see the gulls flying above you. Then sit down beside your little tree and begin to feel her heartbeat. Your heartbeat is her heartbeat.

Feel your tree as she offers you the perspective of joy and delight. Think of those things that bring you sweetness and hope. Remember times that were enjoyable. Allow her energy to fill you with another experience of pure bliss and fun. You may even hear the fairies giggle as you sit within the magic circle of this hardy little tree.

Consider what you are working on right now in your life. Think about where you might be sidestepping or avoiding a challenge or an issue. This may be a time to review and reevaluate your methods or goals. What work needs to be completed before you can move forward? What details must be addressed? What must you let go of? What have you been avoiding?

This tree offers you courage and energy to move forward. Take the steps that you need. Allow her to walk with you. In your mind's eye, see what needs to be done and ask your tree for her sturdiness and strength. Feel her encouragement. She will support you to move toward completion. She promises success and the reward of a job well done if you are willing to put in the work and effort.

Your attention is drawn to the blue sky above you as you hear thunder in the distance. You see a strike of lightning and a distant dark cloud, and suddenly you find yourself immersed in light. White light engulfs you. Breathe deeply and know that you are safe. Be with the light and notice that there is nothing here except love and acceptance. Be in this light for a few moments of silence…

The light delivers you back to the tree and the grassy knoll above the ocean. Give yourself a moment to reflect on your time with the light. What was your experience?

You see a woman walking toward you. She is dressed in a multi-colored woven shawl that is draped over her silver hair. You recognize her as the weaver goddess. As she approaches you, you feel her love and acceptance. She hands you a book. When you open it, you see that the pages are empty.

She says, "It is time to begin anew. I am loosening and unraveling the strands of your old story. Now we begin to write a new chapter as you weave your goals and aspirations and leave behind blockages and fears. This book is full of newly woven strands of light and genius, beauty, and aspiration. The thorny problems and roadblocks are no longer part of this journey."

She speaks more words in the language of light and you hear harp music in the background. She blesses you, kisses both sides of your cheeks, and looks deeply into your eyes. As she begins to turn to walk away, give her your gratitude.

Take your time saying goodbye to the grassy knoll, the ocean, the blue sky, and the sturdy little Spindle. Thank her for her teachings. She reminds you to lighten up and enjoy yourself more. Know that you can return to this place, this tree, the light, and the Goddess anytime you so desire.

Slowly return to the present. Ground and center. Thank your helpers for their protection and guidance and close the portal with your intention.

Sharing

Go around the circle and ask participants to share their thoughts about the Spindle meditation. Were they able to visualize the steps it will take to complete a task? What was their experience with the light? What was their experience with the weaver goddess?

Activity: Titling Journals for Creating New Stories

Have the participants take out their new journals and say, "These are your new stories. The words that you write in this book are to create beauty, peace, love, art, and truth. Light flows within these pages. Here you will write about your inner work, divination, and inspiration. The goddess of weaving has gifted you the energy to create a new story if you so choose. She asks you to put your attention toward the light. She asks you to write about your goals and aspirations in the light of acceptance, courage, and love."

Ask participants to think about the goals and aspirations that the little tree encouraged them to fulfill. Then ask them to create a title for their new journal. Give them a minute to write this title on the first page.

Sharing

Go around the circle and have participants read their journal title. Ask participants to tell the group what they plan to use the journal for. Have them share their goals and aspirations.

Sing

Choose songs that have to do with the sun, spiritual light, the Goddess, or weaving. I suggest "Spiraling into the Center" by Lorna Kohler, "Spirit Above Me" by Moving Breath, "Sundancer," and "Sweet Surrender" by Flight of the Hawk.

Ending

Give gratitude for the Spindle and her guides, totems, and helpers. Ask that the portal be closed and release the directions.

A Spindle Story: Light, Fulfillment, and Weaving Life

The Spindle tree and the Oir are all about light. I am talking about the kind of white light that occurs during a thunderstorm, when the whole sky becomes a flash of light. A lightning strike is sudden and dramatic; insights can be sudden and dramatic in the same way. I am also talking about a lightness of being and the fact that we are all light beings and can share our light. We know the life-giving light of our sun, and we know the face of God or Goddess as light. I experience light as pure consciousness.

I can say truthfully that I had an experience of "standing in the light," and it was a precious and elevating event. This experience happened on my first trip to Egypt in 2007, when I was visiting Seti's Tomb in the Valley of the Kings. I was a member of a tour group of eighteen travelers, and we were lucky to have a private two-hour visit in this special place.

We descended down a dark, sloping corridor that led to the tomb. As we reached the bottom of the corridor, a sense of relief washed over me as coolness touched my skin. It was dim and chilly, a welcome contrast to the hundred-degree heat and glaring sun in the valley above.

As we entered the main gallery, I could have sworn I heard a voice greet me as "the tree lady." I've done healing work with trees for many years, but I'd never thought of myself as "the tree lady," and this was the last place I expected to hear such a greeting. I was thrilled to have been recognized by the energies of the tomb, but I was also caught off guard. I chalked it up to heat, excitement, and a vivid imagination.

As we settled in to do our ceremony, I sat on the stairs and leaned against one of the supporting pillars. The assistive lights were turned off and we were enveloped in total darkness. I ignored my instinct to feel fear or panic. A young man who was traveling with us began playing his handheld harp and with the angelic music, I became calm and receptive. We toned together, making the sound of ohm, and our two leaders began to take us on a guided meditation.

I remember traveling to the top of the great pyramid in my mind's eye, then traveling from there to the stars that form the belt of Orion. There I found a doorway, and as I moved through it, I entered a space of brilliant white light that went on forever in all directions. At that moment, I found myself immersed in that pure light. As I stood there, I felt love, acceptance, and a sense of oneness. It is hard to explain, but I experienced a great sense of fulfillment, sudden illumination, and revelation. I lost track of time and space. I stood in joy, peace, and unity. Who would believe that visiting an Egyptian pharaoh's dark tomb could be an experience of light? Then I heard, *Be open to all possibilities. Experience and remember this holy vibration. When you remember this place, you will remember this expanse, this light, this bliss, and this love. Let this sacred white light reform you.*

Whenever I question myself or the reality of spirit, I remember this tomb and this experience, and the presence of that intelligence and love fills me once again. If I forget this state of being, all I have to do is return to the memory of standing in that special place, absorbing that incredible energy. I can hear the words again and I see myself in the light. I reopen to my full potential as a spiritual being on the planet with work to do as a light-bearer. I remember that I want to share this light that was shared with me.

I am reminded that there are places all over the world where we can more easily communicate with divinity and access spiritual realms. You don't have to visit Egypt or Ireland, although these are wonderful places for spiritual revelation. There are places closer to home: the trees in your neighborhood represent portals of light and are much more accessible. In fact, it was an experience with an apple tree in my backyard almost thirty years ago that led me to work with trees in the first place.

I had a colicky baby that never slept and a husband who preferred to have his wife care for him rather than the other way around. In a moment of upset and intense emotional need, I went to the apple tree in my backyard, sat at her base, put my arms around her, and asked her for help. To my surprise, I felt a response. She sent me what I needed: an outpouring of mothering energy, a reassurance that everything was going to be all right. I sensed her love and support, and I received her energetic nourishment. I actually felt the tree respond through my hands and body as I hugged her and telepathically heard her sweet words. When I realized I could communicate with trees, it was one of the most lovely, unexpected moments. This experience opened up the world to me in ways I could not even understand at the time. This sudden insight and illumination was one of my Spindle moments, even though it was an apple tree that was one of my first tree teachers. The truth is that the door at your heart is the access point for traveling anywhere, especially for traveling for expanded awareness, and there are trees everywhere that are willing to communicate with you.

I am ever grateful for my Spindle moments. I do not have a Spindle tree in my neighborhood in Seattle, so when I first began studying the Spindle, I had to find pictures online and in books. I read as much as I could about her. This is how I came to know her. I always do this when I can't find the actual tree that I am studying. I also meditate, picturing the tree in my mind and taking the time to form a relationship. It is amazing to me how accessible the spirits of the trees are. Again, you can gain access to their world through your intention, attention, respect, and appreciation.

The Spindle teaches about the same spiritual light that I experienced in the tomb in Egypt. She teaches about the fulfillment that is offered by this light. And if we are lucky enough to have experiences with the light that take us outside of our ordinary reality, this sturdy little tree asks us a sobering question: What will we do with these sudden insights and awakenings? How do we use these greater understandings of our true nature and our essential lightness of being? What can we do with this illumination and enlightenment?

It was that Spindle moment with my apple tree over thirty years ago, tucked away in my heart, that prompted me to learn about the tree teachings. And after my journey to Egypt, I began to teach what I had learned about the tree alphabet. I began to write books. I gave talks. I counseled others. I took the leap and moved beyond my comfort zone. All of us start somewhere. I think it is the light that woke me up, and the Spindle that asked me to make what I had experienced tangible and helpful. She asked me to do something with my experience.

This makes me think about the fabric that is ordinary reality. Moment to moment and day to day, we create life through our thoughts, emotions, beliefs, and actions. The Spindle invites us to think about destiny and encourages us to reweave a new story that is more inclusive, loving, and accepting with the assistance of higher dimensions of love and light. This is something that we all can do on a daily basis. It is like taking out the garbage. Simply pull out the strands that aren't working and weave, knit, and sew new ones that hold greater light and possibility. The Spindle asks us to take our desires seriously. The light is prompting us to share ideas to create beauty and make a better world. She wants us to wake up to the fact that we are the creators of our reality.

The Spindle also asks us to complete tasks we have begun. Sometimes in the middle of a project, we give up and say it is too hard or too demanding. The Spindle reminds us of the value of sticking to a task and working until it is done to the best of our ability. When I was working to self-publish my book *Nazmy: Love Is My Religion*, I was in way over my head. Everything was a learning experience, and it took a lot of resolve and determination to keep going. The Spindle's teaching helped immensely. My larger purpose was to share the incredible work that one man was doing to help create peace and understanding between Westerners and his beloved Egypt through spiritual travel. But I really had to dig deep to get the project done. Delays, frustrations, and then the huge task of self-formatting wasn't even in my wheelhouse. It often felt like the story of David and Goliath—impossible. Yet, I kept returning to the purpose: to tell an inspiring story, to share the love of my dear friend Mr. Nazmy.

I think of the little Spindle growing by the sea withstanding the wind. We too can feel as if the wind is blowing too hard—that in bending, we may break. Yet with patience and fortitude, I completed my book and Mr. Nazmy got to see it before he died in August of 2018. I have no words to express how glad I am that I didn't give up. And I love the book. I am proud of it.

Do you have a similar story? Is there something that you are working on that you feel you will never complete? Do you feel like your work isn't good enough or like you don't have the resources you need? I want you to invoke the energy of this dear little Spindle tree. Imagine that this small, sturdy tree is standing next to you, providing you with patience, as you work on your project. Anything worthwhile takes time, effort, and persistence. I often felt like giving up on my book, but I kept my eyes on the prize. I focused on my reason for doing the project in the first place, and it was worth every difficult moment.

Many words ring true for me when I think of the little Spindle tree. She is hardy and yet can be worked with. She represents light and love. She encourages you to create and weave the destiny that you really want. Her teachings are about fulfillment. She encourages persistence in a task. She promises a sense of deep satisfaction when you have completed work to the best of your ability.

As I write this, I think of my son. As a baby, he was so demanding, and now he is almost forty. Raising a child takes persistence, and becoming a good mother takes energy and resolve. I am grateful for the Spindle's teachings. I feel a deep sense of satisfaction and fulfillment when I think about raising my son. And although I was not a perfect mother, I am proud of a job well done. Fulfillment was promised, and I can speak to this fact.

When I think of my first Spindle moment so long ago, I am just so grateful. The nourishment and assurance that I received from the apple tree—the mothering that I needed so desperately as a first-time mother, as well as the magic of the enlightening experience with the tree—woke me up to the reality that I could communicate with the natural world. At the time, the tree knew what I needed more than the people around me. Mothers do need deep nourishing. Communities used to understand this better. Once again, I am reminded of the love and support that is available to us via the natural world. The spirits of the trees are grateful to us for the carbon dioxide that we breathe out. I wish we could be more grateful to them, not only for the oxygen they provide us, but for their incredible giving on so many levels.

Make the little Spindle tree your friend and she will help you in your plans, desires, and projects. She can impart the spirit of endurance and resolve that can help you complete any work that you take on, be it writing a book, painting a picture, cleaning the house, or raising a child. While you are sticking to a task, the Spindle can help you find lightness in the process. She encourages you to create kind moments that become part of the fabric of your reality. Most importantly, she will remind you to keep weaving your life as a creation of beauty.

UILLEAND~HONEYSUCKLE

Ogham: Uilleand (Ull-enth), Ui, P, Pe: ✕

Keywords: Finding your way to the center of self, discriminating what is false from what is worthwhile and useful on your spiritual path, steps to finding inner authenticity and knowledge, fragrance, seeking, hidden secrets, protecting what is sacred

Totems: The lapwing or peewit, hummingbird, bee, moth

Guides and Deities: The hermit; the crone; the medicine woman

Season: Spring

Practical Guidance: Ignore the distractions. Stay true to your own beliefs and principles.

Information: The Ogham symbol for the Uilleand/Honeysuckle is the crossbones formed by crossing the index and middle fingers of each hand, and it stands for Ui, Pe, and P. Honeysuckle flowers attract hummingbirds and bees; the scent is lovely. Her totems are the lapwing/peewit, hummingbird, moth, and bee.

Honeysuckle represents seeking and insight. This vine is about secrets, investigation into what is hidden, and protecting what is sacred. Her guides are the crone or the hermit. This vine helps us to seek light and return to our true nature. Honeysuckle can connect us to our true purpose. She is represented by the design of the labyrinth, our DNA, and the helix. The labyrinth represents the pathway into the inner life. The hermit or crone holds the lantern as you make your way into yourself. This is a journey that one must take alone. This vine encourages you to do so because there are many treasures to be found within.

This vine has to do with the self and the search for inner knowledge. The Honeysuckle helps us to see the false from the true and to choose what is worthwhile and useful to us. This woodbine is an ally that provides you with protection and reminds you to stay true to yourself. Although there are many distractions, this vine symbolizes a focused journey into the self and the soul. It signifies the spiritual journey and it encourages us to keep learning, expressing our true nature, and evolving.

Perhaps you are feeling insecure. This is a state of mind that can be lovingly addressed. True security has nothing to do with failure or success in the world, but rather with recognizing your true nature, which is already perfect and whole. If you are feeling less than, it is time for prayer or inner renewal. You may be burned out or feel lost. You may be leaning on the outside world too much for applause and appreciation, or you may be overly dependent upon the recognition of another. Or perhaps your inner critic never gives you a break. It is time to circle back into yourself. It may be time to take a class or seek a spiritual teacher or choose books that remind you of who you truly are.

Uilleand/Honeysuckle Ceremony

Timing for the Ceremony

Around May 1 and Beltane

Purpose

To seek the light and return to our true nature. To connect to our true purpose. Renewal after an exhausting endeavor or period of work or study. To return to center.

Preparation

Prepare the altar to honor the Uilleand/U ogham and the Honeysuckle.

Welcome and Greetings

Welcome the energy of the Honeysuckle. Introduce yourself and go around the circle, having each participant share their name and why they came to the circle. Have them close their eyes and share a moment of silence to prepare for the ceremony.

Call the Directions

Call in the energy of the Honeysuckle. Call in the bird and bee energies. Invite in the crone and medicine elders to help enlighten the group.

Teachings

Honeysuckle is a climbing, twisty woodbine. She begins to blossom before the Spring Equinox and her blossoms can range from white, yellow, and pink to purple and scarlet. She attracts hummingbirds and bees. She is all about sweetness; her fragrance is a gift. She encourages us to follow the sweet fragrance of the heart, avoid distraction, and move toward the light. Ivy represents the labyrinth of growth into our center and out again, and Honeysuckle represents the lantern to light our path. It is not just about getting to the destination—it is about the quality of the moments that you are creating as you do so. What are you attracting? What are you creating?

And how are you going about the process of that creation? What sweetness do you share that is nourishment for others? This plant will help us to focus and ignore distractions. She offers help so you can align with yourself and what is worthy and useful on your soul's path. The Honeysuckle creates a delightful scent that stirs the heart. Her flower is beautiful. She encourages you to become like the Honeysuckle flower, creating and sharing beauty all around you.

Sing

Choose songs that honor the light, spring, nature, and the heart. I suggest "Sweet Surrender" by Flight of the Hawk.

Chant

> What is the teaching of the Honeysuckle? The fertile secrets of
> the soul lie within.
> Our bliss comes from opening our hearts and offering compassion.
> Behold! What we seek lies within our heart's center.
> And we follow her woodbine path as she leads us to our authentic
> self.
> She asks us to protect and nurture what is sacred.
> What is the teaching of the Honeysuckle? Create sweetness and
> share it with others.

Guided Meditation

Ask each participant to invite in their personal totems, guides, deities, and angels to protect them and help them as they move into their astral body and travel through the portal to other dimensions. (If you are working solo, it is important to set up protections as you open doors into other realms and to close them with gratitude when you return.) Remind your group to be responsible. If they do not like something that is happening in the meditation, they can return to their bodies at any time and close the portal with their intention.

Imagine yourself in a little courtyard that is surrounded by a wall of beautiful Honeysuckle. There is a bench for you to sit down. It is a bright, sunny day and you feel the sun warm your face. As you take a moment to adjust to your garden environment, you breathe in the lovely fragrance. You hear the buzz of the bees and see a few hummingbirds flit in and around the blossoms of the Honeysuckle. You are grateful for the beauty and pleasure of your interaction with this lovely plant and this hidden healing space.

The Honeysuckle also offers light. Thus, this is a place of beauty and renewal. Any need for darkness fades away. You feel welcomed and safe, and you know that this is a place where you can be yourself. There is no need to hide. You feel loved and appreciated. Feel the protection and the solitude offered here. Give your gratitude.

Ask the plant for information about your true purpose. Who are you really? Listen to her messages. What are her revelations about your true nature and purpose? Be willing to receive...

Then the Honeysuckle says, "You are an expression of divinity. There is no one in the universe like you. You are a star shining in the sky, and you are a gift to the world that you find yourself in now. You may have lost your way, forgotten lessons learned, or turned your back on all that is good. No worries. In this moment you are returning to your true nature. You are facing the light and the love of goodness. Receive it as you are made up of it. You can never divest yourself of it. Breathe in the kindness, the forgiveness, and the acceptance. Just be yourself now and let the rest go. You are enough. You come from the light, you live light, and you will return to the light. It can be no other."

Breathe in the message from the Honeysuckle. Allow yourself to be immersed in the unconditional love she offers. Take your time with this…

When you feel complete, it is time to return. Give your gratitude to the Honeysuckle. Then ground, center, and open your eyes. Thank your helpers for their protection and guidance and close the portal with your intention.

Sharing

Have your participants share their experiences with the Honeysuckle. What was revealed about their individual purpose as they received guidance from the Honeysuckle? Were they able to take in the love offered from the Honeysuckle? If so, what did it feel like?

Activity: A Discussion about Authentic Sharing versus Gossiping

One of the keywords for the Honeysuckle is hidden secrets. Lead a discussion about the nature of secrets.

Sometimes we keep secrets close to our hearts because they hold sacred information. In this way, Pagan and indigenous traditions were kept safe after the encroachment of Christianity. Spirituality can also be secretive in nature; many keep their spiritual names secret to protect their energy, for example.

Many people keep secrets because we want to avoid being judged, but holding onto secrets can cost us. There are also the secrets that we keep to ourselves because we are ashamed. Yet, secrets of abuse and wounding need to be shared in order to heal. But we must carefully choose who we share them with—not all listeners honor secrets. Therapists are legally required to keep their clients' secrets unless the secret is about harm to self or others, but many people do not go to a therapist. Instead, they talk to a close friend or a family member. If we are told a secret, we can honor the secret by keeping it close to our hearts.

Speaking about someone can be cruel depending on why we are choosing to share. Distinguish between authentic sharing and gossiping. Sometimes we need to vent, and other times we are just adding to the problem. Encourage a conversation about when to share secrets, when to release them, and when to keep them.

Also talk about the Mysteries. We have so many questions. We seek answers. Sometimes we hold our deepest spiritual beliefs and knowledge secret to protect them. This has been done for eons; in fact, this is how so much ancient knowledge was protected. It was only passed on to those that could honor it and hold it as sacred. We are lucky to live in a time when we have access to so much ancient knowledge, teachers, and wisdom and we have the freedom to practice our individual spiritual expressions.

Sing

Choose songs that honor the Mysteries. I suggest "Where I Sit is Holy" by Shaina Noll and Russell Walden.

Ending

Give your gratitude to the teachings and blessings of the Honeysuckle as well as her totems, guides, and deities. Give your gratitude for the Mysteries. Sing "We Are a Circle" by Rick Hamouris. Close the portal and release the directions.

A Honeysuckle Story:
Secrets and Protecting What Is Sacred

Honeysuckle was a new plant for me to work with, as I usually focus on the first fifteen trees of the Celtic tree calendar. After I studied and wrote about the plant, I took a walk with my husband. As we were walking down the block, we noticed a lovely fragrance. I asked him if he recognized the scent. He said, "Yes, it is Honeysuckle," and there it was! He showed me a trellis of white flowers growing along twisty woodbine stems at the top of a metal fence enclosing a yard. We took pictures. I was amazed that I had never noticed this plant before because we passed by it all the time. This experience is common when I start focusing on a specific tree or shrub. As soon as I begin to study it, I find it! It's magic!

This plant is all about creating sweetness in our lives. It is also about creating safe havens. Thus, protection is a theme. The plant offers food and protection for birds, insects, and bees. It sets up boundaries. It reminds us to protect what is most sacred to us and to take care of the flora and fauna that we steward.

The Honeysuckle is the light that our helpers and guides shine for us as we begin the journey into our center to discover our true authentic selves. We can trust the light as we uncover our own secrets and wounding that keeps us stuck and afraid. At the center is power, truth, and regeneration. We find that we are truly enough. Healing is offered if we take the journey.

When you undertake such inner work, you begin an alchemical process. You are changing from base consciousness—identified with the desires of the ego and the conditioning of your milieu—to a golden consciousness of compassion and care that is identified with divinity. While on this journey I recommend journaling and creating art, music, and poetry. It is important to express what you are experiencing. You are chronicling your own transformation. This also may be an important time to find a therapist to support you. Don't forget that you have your own support system in the unseen realms that you can lean on; ask them for help, as they cannot participate in your healing without your permission. I have often found that the plant and tree spirits offer the best comfort and support because they are elemental, and they have a deep knowing without speaking. They are deep listeners and witnesses, and they are willing to provide the perfect energetic prescription.

The Honeysuckle is also about secrets, and she gives us a blue-print for how to handle secrets. Foremost is the mystery. Things are hidden on purpose to protect them from improper use or the ego's need to accumulate power. If you seek to develop a practice that connects you to the spiritual dimensions, it is best not to dabble or skim over the teachings. In-depth study and devoting time to the practice is important; do not skip steps. If we misuse our power to control others or merely to seek out our own desires, it can backfire. The rules of karma are in play. The mystery will reveal itself to the truth seekers if they remain honest and humble. When to share this knowledge and with whom is a matter of discrimination and comes with maturity and wisdom.

Other kinds of secrets can be classified as gossip. Gossip has no good purpose and simply perpetuates an environment of chaos, harm, and distrust. If you can talk about someone with another, they can also talk about you. Gossiping may help get thoughts and feelings off our chests, but it also has an aftertaste: guilt. I always feel guilty when I gossip about someone I love. It takes a certain discipline to decline from participating in such behavior, yet it is worth it as you create an environment of kindness, empathy, and trust. You are helping build a world of respect, integrity, and health.

With that being said, I do sometimes share with a trusted friend when I am having difficulties with someone. I preface the conversation by saying that I need some guidance about my need to judge or my need to criticize. In this way, I am addressing my own negative tendencies. Thus, the light is on me, not on another. I have found addressing the challenges that I am having with friends or family in this way can be very helpful. I can even strategize a way to deal with the person that is more positive and helpful.

And then there are your own secrets. Many are kept in the dark because of a sense of shame and humiliation. If they are not released into the daylight, they wound and fester and mess with your life.

Finding a therapist, minister, or very trusted friend to tell these stories to can be important to the healing process. Many of us feel stories of abuse are our fault, but we soon discover that is not true. And many of us have hurt others and are afraid to disclose these secrets because we do not want to be judged. Your intuition is important here. Only tell these kinds of secrets to someone that is very trustworthy.

Others may choose to share their most intimate situations and challenges with you. These are an honor to keep close to your chest. Divulging someone else's secret is a violation and may hurt the person that has shared with you. It is just not worth it. Once I told a secret that I was meant to respect, and I really hurt and betrayed a dearly loved friend. I lost his friendship because I betrayed his trust. It was an awful lesson to learn, and I still miss him even after thirty years. At the time, I just couldn't carry the weight of his secret. If I could do it over again, I would talk to him about how I was feeling and see what we could do about it together. One of my biggest regrets is not keeping this secret sacred. I have learned from my mistakes. It is awful to betray someone you care about in this way.

In a way, my spiritual path is held secret. I don't go around talking about it all the time. When there is a need, I reveal what I know and believe. I do share with my clients, family, and friends. Yet, I hold my beliefs close because I am not interested in being judged by the more conservative world that I live in. Writing books is one way to share, and I have discovered that others find it helpful and inspirational. This is a great blessing.

Think about your particular gifts and how you share them. Think about the sweetness that you create in your life. Feel gratitude for the gifts that have been bestowed to you. Consider this an encouragement to share your light. The Honeysuckle reminds us to create light, love, and beauty. That means that we are invited to think before we act or speak. Words have power.

I like to chant these words (adapted from "Spirit All Around Me," a traditional song put to music by Mujiba Cabugos) to help me remember to create sweetness:

> *I create beauty above me.*
> *I create beauty below me.*
> *I create beauty before me.*
> *I create beauty behind me.*
> *I create beauty all around me.*
> *I am the beauty that I create.*

PHAGOS–BEECH

Ogham: Phagos, Io, Ph: ᚘ

Keywords: Generations, books, ancient knowledge, higher dimensions of love and understanding, reading the past, present, and future

Totems: Owl, snake, Tree of Knowledge

Guides and Deities: The Great Mother; Merlin; Ogma; Danu; elders; shamans; writers, scholars, and historians; medicine men and women; seers

Season: Summer

Practical Guidance: Guidance from the past can help you gain insight. Seek wisdom.

Information: The Phagos/Beech is all about wisdom, generations, the ancestors, ancient knowledge, enlightened information, and ancient spells, texts, scrolls, and books. Her totems are the snake and the owl, and her deities are the Great Mother goddesses, crones, ancestors, archangels, Merlin, Thoth (Egypt), and spiritual teachers. The Ogham symbol for the Phagos/Beech is the hook. It represents the vowel sound Io and the consonant combination sound of Ph. A good time to include this tree may be at the fire celebration of Lammas on August 1. Here we honor the fullness of summer and give gratitude for abundance and fulfillment. We honor the mother aspect of the Goddess.

The Beech helps us connect to wisdom and guidance. Pay attention to advice, especially if it comes from elders and revered teachers in your life. Knowledge from the past may help you avoid mistakes in the future. Open yourself up to receiving information from your environment. The Beech helps to inform the psychic or the seer, those that read the oracles. This tree represents a dive into the deep mystery that contains all knowledge and has access to the past, present, and future. This library, if you will, is also known as the Akashic Records. The information that is stored here can be accessed through a wise person, a book, a dream, or intuition. It may come in the form of an astrological reading or a tarot reading. We may ask the I Ching, tarot, runes, the fews of the Ogham, or other cards systems for wisdom and guidance. I often use a pendulum to access this place of knowing when I need to make a decision and am unsure of what to do. There are other forms of guidance as well; I have developed what I call Tree Readings for my clients, where I tune into a tree, listen deeply to its message, and then share this message in the reading. Sometimes, when I am seeking guidance and receive an answer I am unsure about, I will use another method and ask the same question. Invariably, I get similar guidance.

All of these systems tap into the well of knowledge, past, present, and future. It is this library that allows the oracle to inform and guide us. Of course, it is always prudent to seek seers, readers, healers, and psychics that are responsible and reputable. In this sense, I always trust the Beech. It doesn't have a human agenda, it is wise and knowing, and it considers how best to share with me and how best to guide me. Again, I often prefer the counsel of the trees over any human, yet I do have reputable readers that I go to and that I respect.

Another aspect of the Beech tree is its support for scholars and students. This tree invites you to study, do research, or gather information. The Beech will help you in any field of study. It provides energy for the long hours of diligence, sacrifice, and hard work that it takes to get a degree, become an expert, or become proficient at a profession. The Beech will support you through internships, testing and evaluation processes, licensing processes, graduate programs, and intense periods of scholastic study, research, and writing. I certainly embraced the energy of the Beech when I was in graduate school. I have often asked that the energy of the great Beech be with my daughter, who has just completed law school. What a long and intense process that was for her, but she remained steady and resolved, just like the wise Beech.

If you are beginning a project, this tree offers you stability and a strong foundation. This tree also offers you grounding energy. It can provide and create sacred space for you. When you are overwhelmed or frazzled, call on the Beech to ground you and allow that extra energy to return to the earth. She will help you return to your endeavor with renewed energy. This can be especially important when you are challenged to follow through on the hard work that is necessary to reach your goals; she will help you stay on track.

The Beech is full of the ancient mysteries of the British Isles. If you are embodying the energy of the Beech, you might be drawn to ancient information. You might seek answers from the ancient past or lost wisdom. Perhaps you seek guidance and information from your elders. You might research your own lineage and ancestry.

Many are drawn to systems of information that connect to the mystery: the library of the past, present, and future. I know I was. I love symbols and art, so I was drawn to tarot and astrology in my twenties. I have studied the I Ching, the Tree of Life, runes, hieroglyphs, and the Ogham. I found great pleasure in the folklore of the British Isles and in the British mysteries, as well as the Egyptian mysteries. I was drawn to research material that was outside the box of my more conventional world. I was yearning for deeper answers to my questions about the meaning of my life. I learned from my dreams, intuition, and art. I developed a dialogue with wisdom and with my own guides, totems, and deities. I found my natural home with the trees and settled on developing a spiritual practice based on the Ogham. I am especially grateful for the teachings of the Beech, which restored my faith in the ancient nature teachings that respect the web of life, and for her encouragement. I have always felt that this tree backed my studies, research, and writing.

This tree may prompt you to take up a position of authority in your community as a teacher, counselor, or civic leader. You may be drawn to public service or a position of authority in larger systems like law and justice, religion, journalism, politics, or medicine. In other words, you are drawn to use your wisdom to guide and serve others. You may be drawn to share your wisdom as a healer, shaman, or oracular reader. You may be called to become an orator or a writer, or you may support the publication of such work. You may take on apprenticeships in essential work, be it as an electrician, plumber, or builder. Sharing knowledge, wisdom, and skill—all of this is Beech work.

Phagos/Beech Ceremony

Timing for the Ceremony
Around August 1 and Lammas

Purpose
To connect to wisdom. To learn how to read objects, called *psychometry*. To seek guidance—especially now, because of the difficulties we are experiencing on Earth.

Preparation

Prepare the altar to honor the Phagos ogham and the Beech. Fill a bowl with small items to be used in a later activity. Small item ideas include a feather, a gemstone, a child's toy, a coin, a piece of jewelry, a knickknack, etc.

Welcome and Greetings

Welcome the energy of the Beech. Introduce yourself and go around the circle, having each participant share their name and why they came to the circle. Have them close their eyes and share a moment of silence to prepare for the ceremony.

Call the Directions

Call in the energy of the Beech. Call in the elders, the healers, the wise ones, and the ancestors. Invite in the wisdom of the ages. Call in the Great Goddess (you may choose to call her by many names). Call in the owl and snake energies.

Teachings

The Beech connects you to wisdom. She is traditionally called the queen of the woods and is associated with snake wisdom and earth energies. She is loved by the Great Goddess. The Beech is associated with ancient learning and knowledge. In fact, the first runes and ogham were said to be carved on Beech wood. She is sacred to Ogma, the god of eloquence, as well as the goddess Danu, the goddess of knowledge and learning. She has a close association with magic and magical lore. She enjoys spoken spells and litanies. Inviting in her energy increases tolerance, compassion, and gentleness and draws in the unconditional love of the Great Goddess.

Beech had to do with ancient knowledge revealed through old objects, places, and writings. When you invite in the energy of the

Beech, you may feel motivated to do research or study, or you may be drawn to mythology or the study of ancient people and their beliefs. You may be drawn to certain places and cultures.

The Beech reminds you that the wisdom from the ancient past can offer insight and help you build a solid foundation for your life. Perhaps you are at a place where lost wisdom is needed. Perhaps you are looking for survival skills. Seek advice from elders, teachers, ancestors, ancient sources, and lineages. You may seek guidance from the oracle who taps into the deep well of wisdom and knowledge that is found in the mystery.

Due to the world's climate crises—and 2020's worldwide pandemic—we will be forced to find more holistic ways to live. Seek the wisdom of the snake, the owl, and the priestess of the Beech. Invite in the wisdom of the Beech itself. Perhaps this is what the ancient people had to do as they discovered what plants to use for their well-being. Perhaps this is how they found their water and food sources. When we pray and seek, information will be given. We need new solutions, and they may actually be based on ancient insight. When we seek guidance, we may be presented with ideas, inventions, and recovery processes that are based on earth energy and earth wisdom. Perhaps the restoration of our land, soil, air, and water lie in this ancient knowing. Remembering that the web of life was created in balance, and this is the key to understanding our recovery. The Beech offers us access to ancient knowing. Listen deeply whenever you seek wisdom from this tree.

Activity: Playing with Psychometry

With the help of the Beech, have your participants play with psychometry, the art of reading objects and telling their story. Show participants your prepared bowl of small objects. Tell them that each object in the bowl has a spiritual message for the group.

Pass the bowl around the circle. Have each participant choose an item and take it from the bowl. After each participant has their object, have them close their eyes. Ask them to feel into the object and receive its special message. Let a few minutes pass. Then go around the circle and have each participant share the spiritual message that came to them as they held their object.

This is a fun activity meant to acquaint each participant with their own inner knowledge and the great knowledge of the Beech. Both tap into the mystery. The teaching is that our intuition, our inner knowing, is one of our best and truest senses. The more we use it, the stronger it gets, and we can make a habit of relying on its assistance.

Sing

Choose songs that honor ancient wisdom or the Great Goddess. I suggest "Blood of the Ancients" by Ellen Klaver or "We All Come from the Goddess" by Moving Breath.

Chant

> *What is the teaching of the Beech? Seek ancient wisdom.*
> *The ancestors and those of higher realms of love and understanding support you.*
> *Behold! Ask and you shall receive.*
> *There is wisdom to be found in the stories and the legends of your own homelands and your ancestors.*
> *Your survival depends on staying close to nature and listening to her messages.*
> *What is the teaching of the Beech? The Great Mother Goddess will help you.*

Guided Meditation

Ask each participant to invite in their personal totems, guides, deities, and angels to protect them and help them as they move into their astral body and travel through the portal to other dimensions. (If you are working solo, it is important to set up protections as you open doors into other realms and to close them with gratitude when you return.) Remind your group to be responsible. If they do not like something that is happening in the meditation, they can return to their bodies at any time and close the portal with their intention.

As you close your eyes, allow yourself to travel until you are in the midst of an old Beech grove. At the center of the grove sits a large, commanding Beech tree. You recognize it as the Tree of Knowledge. This is a mighty, ancient site, and you can feel the power of ancient wisdom here. Sit down in the center of the grove at the foot of this large tree and allow yourself to rest within the web of knowledge…

The keepers of the grove come close. One is an earth snake that side winds up to you and communicates to you that there is no need to be afraid, as she is an ally. She sends calming vibrations. Then she coils herself close to you and waits patiently, sending you comfort and grounding. The other keeper of the grove, a snowy owl, comes to a low tree branch just above you and looks at you with her huge yellow eyes. She gives you a hoot of welcome.

From the trees comes a lady, a priestess, a goddess. She is singing and playing a small hand harp that she carries in her left hand. Her song is like a beautiful poem, and you fall under her loving spell.

She comes before you and says, "Greetings! I have been sent from the Great Goddess herself. I am the priestess of this Beech grove and the protector of our great wisdom tree here at the center. I come to welcome you to this place of legendary wisdom. As you sit at the foot of this great tree and look around this ancient grove, you can feel the power of this place. These trees hold the wisdom of our ancient ones. They know all of the questions and the answers, and they know all the stories, past, present, and future.

"We know that there are many challenges and dilemmas that you are facing at this time. Do not despair. We will guide you through this. Be kind to one another. We will impart the knowledge and wisdom that you need and that you are seeking. Stay in the moment. It is enough for right now to stay present, one day at a time. Rest assured.

"I come to imbue you with the love, the compassion, and the gentle support of our Goddess." She bends down to where you are sitting and places her right hand upon your heart. You immediately feel her transmission…

As for the challenges and dilemmas that you are facing, you immediately have the courage and the wherewithal to face them. Wisdom and reassurance come to you, blessed by the Goddess and shared by the grove. You know that you can prevail no matter what your troubles are. Breathe this in deeply. Stay with this knowing for a moment…

You feel loved and held and encouraged. You know that you can continue to pursue your goals and aspirations—especially if they support and respect nature and are helpful to others—because they are blessed by the Great Goddess and the ancestors of this place.

Give your gratitude to this priestess, the Great Goddess, the snake and the owl, the ancestors, the grand central tree, and the grove of Beech. Give your gratitude for the knowledge and wisdom that rests here. Know that you can return to this place anytime. As your questions arise, the goddess of this grove will help you move through challenging times step-by-step.

When you are ready, return to the present and ground and center. Thank your helpers for their protection and guidance and close the portal with your intention.

Sharing

Have the participants share their experiences from the Beech meditation. Have each person share how they are getting through these challenging times. If someone is in need of healing, help, or encouragement, have the group provide energy for them.

Sing

Choose songs that honor those that have gone before us. I suggest "Changing Woman," "Triple Goddess Chant" by Moving Breath, "Like the Old Ones Gone Before," and "Spiraling into the Center" by Lorna Kohler.

Prayers

Go around the circle and have each participant make a prayer for the planet and its healing. Summon the energy of the Great Goddess, the central Tree of Knowledge, and the grove of the Beech. Ask that each person be led and guided to their own wisdom and inner knowing.

Activity: Brainstorming and Creating Ideas for Living Lightly

Go around the circle and brainstorm ideas for changing basic practices and ways of living that most people have grown accustomed to. How can we change our actions so that they are more supportive of the environment? What attitudes and assumptions require change? Share ideas for supporting the earth and living lighter. What can we let go of? What can we stop consuming? How can we reduce our waste? How can we use less water and electricity? What organizations can we lend our time and money to that support the earth and protect her resources?

Ask the group to share resources about living an eco-friendly lifestyle. What organizations are doing this work right now? Where can we buy necessary products that are not harmful to the environment?

Where can we buy products that come in eco-friendly packaging? For example, there are sites on the internet where you can buy laundry soap, deodorant, toothpaste, and hair products that are not packaged with plastic. Take notes. Begin to build a list of helpful sites and ways that the group can live more lightly. Share the list with the group and keep building it. Become wisdom scribes for the planet.

Ending

Stand as a grove of Beech trees and tone together. Sing, "We are a circle within a circle, with no beginning and never-ending." Close the portal and release the directions. Open the circle.

A Beech Story: Celtic Spiritual Cosmology, Ireland, and Stewardship

I love to read and study. I must have been a scribe or an ancient wisdom teacher in another life. Perhaps I was a priestess of the woods or an early Christian monk, carefully scribing stories and legends onto a vellum page or inking in the beautiful Celtic lettering and creating the pictures. I love books, paper, pens, and words. I enjoy writing and creating, and it has been my passion to pass on what I know to be true from my own experiences with the Celtic tree alphabet and the calendar. Beech represents ancient knowledge and is a special friend to me, and I have enjoyed every moment working with this teaching.

The Beech is symbolic of this Celtic spiritual cosmology. Because the ancient knowledge was passed down orally, it involved memorization and the use of mnemonic devices as we see in the Ogham, as well as the retelling of stories and the repetition of songs over a long history. The bards and adepts, the initiated scholars and wisdom keepers, the wizards and shamans, and the spiritual elders protected the teachings over time. Later the wisdom and teachings were recorded in scrolls and books, often by educated Catholic monks, although storytellers and musicians kept them alive as well. But what is most important is that this particular wisdom that has been passed down to us over the centuries is meant to help us live well on our planet. It is meant to help us take care of all life on Earth, to protect its resources, and to get along with each other. The Beech represents this wise yet practical knowledge. We need this today more than ever.

To me, the most important teaching of the ancients was their perspective on death, rebirth, and regeneration from season to season and year to year. Their connection to their ancestors and loved ones that had passed through the veil was an important part of their spirituality. To them, death was a doorway into another realm, and they could communicate with those that had made the passage. Their lost loved ones became their guides; they honored them and asked for their council and wisdom. Death was a natural progression, not something to be feared.

I encourage all of us to question our assumptions, our need for denial, and our fear of death and aging. So much of our culture is built on the belief that looking young is something to strive for. So much of our attention and our resources are focused on buying products and activities that are geared toward creating an image of what we think we should look like—with the emphasis on being what we look like, not who we are. Advertising has created a whole new way of being and consuming. It sits on a foundation of waste and greed and is a misuse of our resources. It creates a desire to have an illusionary lifestyle that has nothing to do with our authentic needs. Our creature comforts have become our masters. This is such an outrageous and audacious misuse of our time, attention, and money. It is fundamental mind control. The denial of death and the need for ego-driven, materialistic pleasure drives the need for more money, power, and consumption. This denial obstructs the inner life and our sacred contract with stewarding the planet. This attitude of bigger, better, and more has led us to a great crisis. We are misusing the resources of Mother Earth.

The teachings from the ancients can help us. Celtic cosmology grew out of the observation of the cycles of nature and people's ability to survive, thrive, appreciate, and protect their environments. They created seasonal ceremonies to express their gratitude. They did not take their well-being for granted. They learned how to appreciate all of life as sacred and how to steward the earth and her flora and fauna. Air, water, and land were revered and held sacred. They were in a powerful relationship with Gaia and the web of life.

The pillars that Celtic cosmology stands upon are sourced from the magical vibrancy of Ireland. The people there still connect with the spirit of the land by visiting ancient wells, caves, glens, and forests. There is a deep spiritual mysticism to be found there. Music, story and myth, and poetry run through the veins of the people and are protected and generated by the land, mountains, valleys, rivers, streams, lakes, and sea. It is a rich spirituality that is nature-based and respectful. The unseen world is shared with the seen world and the Divine Spirit is present in every living creature as well as all the aspects of nature. This Celtic feeling is generated from the land of Ireland herself. It is she that provides this deep connection to Source, nature, and the rhythms of her people's lives.

I am so grateful that this Celtic wisdom is available to us. These teachings may not be complete or exactly as they were when the Druids taught them or when the bards told the stories and sang the songs, but the knowledge of reverence and stewardship is still coming forth like a bright spring of clean, clear water bubbling up from the earth. I am grateful to those who teach about this Celtic spirituality in books and through talks and classes. And the internet makes all of this so much more accessible.

I have built a spiritual practice based upon my own interactions with this cosmology. Today my church is a grove, and my teachers are the trees. I want to plant more trees and protect the ones that are alive now; they are the lungs of our planet. I want to live lightly on the earth and conserve and protect her resources. I do not believe that she owes me anything. I do believe, based on these teachings, that it is an honor to be here and that my job is to be a good steward. I teach classes about the Ogham and the trees and offer ceremonies as a way of showing my gratitude. Following the Wheel of the Year and honoring the changing seasons through ritual and ceremony is my way of remembering to show my grateful heart and to say thank you for these blessings. Gratitude is one of the most important practices we utilize when honoring nature.

One can't take up the teachings of the ancestors without facing up to the many lies embedded in our modern lifestyle. It is time to stop our misuse of the earth's resources and return to a way of living that supports and sustains life. Returning to the old ways of gratitude and stewardship is a necessity. The planet doesn't need us to survive, but we certainly need it. We know that we are in survival mode as a species. We have endangered all life on our planet because of our greed and our tendency to foul the nest that we live in. We are being asked to think globally, lessen our carbon footprint, be less materialistic, and share and protect our resources. (After all, why do we really need all this stuff?) We are asked to confront the reality of climate change and global warming. We are asked to change our ways.

My greatest hope is that we return to these lovely tree teachings to help us live in harmony with our natural world and to live in peace with each other as stewards of this paradise. It comes down to the fact that trees give us oxygen and we give them carbon dioxide. We need each other to live. And so, I remind you to protect the land, the water, the air, and your own connection with nature. What good is a teaching if we don't act practically and commit to our stewardship? I encourage you to donate your time and money. Be a warrior for peace and commit to protecting the web of life. This is what the ancients hoped we would do. The trees have our backs. Let's make sure we have theirs.

MOR~SEA

Ogham: Mor, Ae, Xi, X: ▦

Keywords: Rivers, lakes, pools, oceans, the waters of the planet, the rain, tears, homelands and ancestral roots, journeys, mother, spiritual roots, cleansing and purification, honoring emotions, intuition

Totems: Water nymphs, mermaids, all water creatures (dolphin, whale, salmon)

Guides and Deities: Ancestors; gods and goddesses of your homelands; loved ones who have crossed over; goddesses of the moon; Manannán mac Lir, god of the sea; mother goddesses; river goddesses Boand, Sinann, Sequana, Banba, Brigantia, Belisama; the Irish mother goddess Ériu

Season: Summer or fall

Practical Guidance: Trust your feelings and follow your intuition. Connect with your ancestors and loved ones that have crossed over. Protect the waters of the planet.

Information: The Ogham symbol for Mor/Sea is represented by a square of woven fabric: the warp and weft of a shirt of the god

Manannán. It stands for Ae, X, and Xi and represents journeys, maternal links, and the land. This is the one instance in the Ogham where a tree, shrub, or plant is not honored. In this case, we refer to the element of water, to the land we herald from, to the homes of our ancestors, and to our maternal links. Mor is about the oceans, rivers, lakes, and bodies of water on the planet and our need to protect them. Mor represents the mothers of our lineage, the yearning to travel, and the great oceans from which all life was created. Here we honor the waters of the planet, our own blood and body, and the unconscious, our inner child or our lower self (which does not mean that it is less important). This ogham also represents returning to the countries that we herald from, returning to our roots and honoring our family legacies.

The totems are the water nymphs as well as the mermaids and mermen that protect the waters on the planets. Water creatures such as dolphins, whales, and salmon are totems that are willing to share their wisdom. The guides and deities include all the moon gods and goddesses and the Great Mother Goddess herself, with her many names. Manannán mac Lir, the Irish god of the sea and creator of the crane bag, shares his sacred knowledge with us. Your own crane bag holds the sacred tools and teachings that you carry safely within your heart and soul.

Perhaps it is time to take a trip or journey. This could be of a nature that connects you to your ancestral homeland or your spiritual home, or this might indicate that this is time for self-study or studying with a teacher. You might choose shamanism or a form of spirituality that has to do with your heart. This could refer to a spiritual pilgrimage or an inner journey to reconnect with your authentic self for guidance. Take time to connect with your ancestors and ask them for guidance or to help you along your chosen path.

Perhaps you have strayed from your origins, but it is time to realign with the ancestors. You may feel that you are at sea. Take a time out. Stop moving so fast so that you can listen to your own inner guidance. If you are separated or estranged from your family or loved ones, it might be time to reconnect.

Give gratitude for Mother Earth and for the air, the land, and the sea. Give gratitude for your mother and for those women that had a hand in raising you. Be grateful for your maternal links, grandmothers, and great-grandmothers. If you suffer from a female or mother wounding, perhaps it is time for some forgiveness work. Difficult mothers are backward teachers.

There is hardly any human alive today that doesn't have mother or father wounds. Because the Great Mother represents unconditional love, she is the kind path offered for healing. She is not in a rush. Like the water she represents, she flows and brings refreshment. She replenishes the hardened heart places by opening the heart chakra and allowing tears to flow. She is not pushy, makes no demands, and lets you know that your timing is perfect. Every flower must bud on its own terms. She knows that you will flower. With enough constancy and tender concern, even the wildest or the most abused of animals will begin to trust. Our abused and neglected parts respond the same when there is enough ground to feel secure again. To trust again. To proceed and move toward the light.

There is healing to be found in spiritual journeys. Many folks travel to Peru, Egypt, or the British Isles on a spiritual pilgrimage. Here you can connect to your familial roots as well as the spiritual roots that you identify with. These places hold magic and mystery for healing. Mor represents such spiritual pilgrimages.

Mor also supports journeys taken for meditation called *imaginative journeying*. Here you can astral travel any place you so desire. The unconscious is onboard with experiences that will help you heal. Places, totems, ogham, and deities and guides show up for protection and to support your healing; dreams work in the same way. This is the providence of Mor.

Choose to do something for the water on the planet. Perhaps it is time to take a careful look at your attitude toward water. Clean water is endangered, and we are called upon to do everything we can to protect the element of water. Stop buying, using, and throwing away plastic. This stuff is being thrown into our oceans and is making its way into our bodies. Do not use rat poison, weed killers, or other substances that harm our underground water system. Buy local food or organic food that does not rely on the use of glyphosates. Support legislation and legislators that protect our oceans, cut back on how much water you use, and be mindful of what you pour down the drain. Find ways to conserve what you use. One way to do this is to position your gutter drains to run into rain barrels; these barrels will hold the rainwater for you to reuse in your garden. Become a water protector. Without vigilance, there are no guarantees for the water on this planet. If you cannot be one who stands on the front line, give your support however you can. Give your gratitude to Mor and commit to protecting her.

Mor is a magical cauldron of death, rebirth, and healing. The Goddess is the keeper of the cauldron. Place your worries and fears into the cauldron and expect the guidance and light that you require. The Goddess is aware of your problems and concerns, and she is happy to cook them up into a new brew of hope and reward. She is prepared to support you, but you must ask for her help.

The abundance of summer is all about the mother aspect of the Goddess, so summer is a great time for this last ogham's teachings. Anytime you want to do a gratitude ceremony for the waters of the planet, you can turn to Mor. Mor is also about any ceremony that honors the ancestors. You might choose to do a Mor ceremony before a trip, especially if you are taking a spiritual pilgrimage.

Mor/Sea Ceremony

Timing for the Ceremony

Summer, fall, or at the end of your ceremony or study/teaching schedule. Because Mor is the last ogham, we can think about endings and new beginnings. If you are studying the last ten ogham over a period of time, this ogham can represent the end of the study sequence.

Purpose

Honoring the element of water, maternal lineages, or ancestry.

Preparation

Prepare the altar to honor the Sea and the Mor ogham. Set a large glass or crystal bowl of water on your central altar. Place amethysts and other water-safe crystals at the bottom. Have a larger crystal or wand for stirring the waters. Purchase small vials with lids so participants can take blessed water home with them. Prepare or buy small bags that you can give your participants at the end of the ceremony; these will become their crane bags.

Welcome and Greetings

Welcome the energy of the Sea. Introduce yourself and go around the circle, having each participant share their name and why they came to the circle. Have them close their eyes and share a moment of silence to prepare for the ceremony.

Call the Directions

Call the directions and invoke the energies of the Sea (homelands, the waterways of the planet, cleansing). Call in the totems, guides, and deities: water nymphs, the mermaids, sea creatures, goddesses of the moon, Manannán mac Lir, ancestors, and loved ones who have passed on. Invite in the Great Mother Goddess.

Activity: Naming Homelands and Spiritual Affinities

Go around and ask each participant which countries they herald from and which places they have a spiritual affinity for. For example, my relatives on my mother's side come from England, the Isle of Mann, and Cornwall. On my father's side, they come from Germany, Scotland, Ireland, and Wales. My spiritual affinities are Native American, European/Celtic, and Egyptian.

Teachings

This is a ceremony to honor the ancestors and the lands we come from. We also honor the element of water and celebrate our tears, emotions, bodies, and blood. We honor the rivers, creeks, streams, oceans, seas, lakes, streams, pools, and ponds as well as the rain. We honor all the gods and goddesses of the waters. We honor salt water, fresh water, and all the creatures that live in the waters. We honor the rain and the water cycle. We recommit to taking care of our planet. We vow to clean up our waters and to reduce pollution of the waters. Perhaps it is time for our own personal cleaning process, whether it be physical, emotional, relational, or spiritual.

We also honor all that is represented by the element of water: the unconscious, the Mysteries, hidden knowledge, the moon, lunar aspects, and the feminine principle, as well as the motherland. Mor is linked with our place of birth, the lands our ancestors came from, and the moon. Notice what phase the moon is right this moment. Take some time out of your evening routine to look up at the darkened sky and notice the moon. Follow it through the month. The moon represents change, mothering, emotional connection, and nurturance. She is all about our innate desire to help one another. Mor is all about our connections to others and our relationships; this ogham invites us to honor our emotional life and to value our emotions even when they are difficult.

Mor also represents the places that we may have to travel to enhance and support our spiritual journey. The Sea connects us to our maternal line and to the Goddess. All life comes from mothers and the Great Mother aspect of nature. We honor all mothers and the gods and goddesses of the waters. We honor nurturance, tender care, and mothering. We honor emotional support and compassion.

Sing

Sing songs that honor water and the Great Goddess. I suggest "We All Come from the Goddess" by Moving Breath, "The River Is Flowing" by Diana Hildebrand-Hull, and "The Earth, the Air, the Fire, the Water" by Libana.

Chant

> *What is the teaching of Mor, the Sea? Gratitude for the mother.*
> *It is she that gives us life and holds the mystery in her hands.*
> *Behold! She loves us and supports us.*
> *She is our ancestor and our chalice.*
> *She encourages us to take care of our precious land, sea, and air.*
> *What is the teaching of Mor, the Sea? Honor the precious gift*
> *of your life.*

Guided Meditation

Ask each participant to invite in their personal totems, guides, deities, and angels to protect them and help them as they move into their astral body and travel through the portal to other dimensions. (If you are working solo, it is important to set up protections as you open doors into other realms and to close them with gratitude when you return.) Remind your group to be responsible. If they do not like something that is happening in the meditation, they can return to their bodies at any time and close the portal with their intention.

Take a few deep breaths and focus your intention inward. You are going to visit the island of Iona, which is off the west coast of Britain. It is a place of mystery, and it offered a safe haven for the Druidic mystics who were persecuted by the Romans. It is here that you return to Druidic knowledge and training.

The moon is full and the tide is high as you stand upon the beach of the isle of Iona. It is a pure place, with the high wind coming in from the sea before you. The land is specked with strong trees, their twisted trunks shaped by the constant impact of the wind. Take a moment to connect with the earth here in this place. Grow roots down into the sand and feel the resources there at the deepest level; they can guide and sustain you.

You see the goddess of the sea emerge from the water. At first she is a seal, but then she shape-shifts into a beautiful woman draped in green seaweed. She walks up to you. You smell the sharp, tangy aroma of her seaweed dress and the kelp that she wears around her neck. You taste the salty breeze on your lips, and you feel the crisp wind on your face. You watch the ocean waves as they crash upon the beach and then fade back into the sea. You hear the faint, sweet music of the harp and drum, and you feel the goddess's great love.

The sea goddess represents unconditional love. She is your mother and my mother. She is our original home. As she meets you, she points up to the stars and says, "The Milky Way is but a river. As much as you are part of earth, you are also made of stardust. Your parents come from the stars. Thus, you are very much made up of the higher intelligence of the galaxies." Take a moment to take this in…

The goddess takes a large abalone shell from within the sleeve of her seaweed dress, and you see that it is full of water. She asks where your ancestors are from. As you tell her, she touches your forehead with the water in a blessing. She asks you where you live now. While you answer, she touches your forehead again and blesses the ancient ones of the place where you reside. She then asks, "Where are the places on earth that you love the most?" She blesses those places and their teachings by touching your forehead. She asks you where you want to travel. And as she touches your forehead, she blesses those places.

Then she looks you right in the eye and sends you a transmission of her unconditional love. Be willing to receive. Just soak it in and let it restore you. Breathe deeply and feel her blessing. If you have a question or concern, now is the time. Talk to the goddess, as she is very willing to help you…

When you feel complete, you may thank her and offer her a gift. Perhaps you are willing to offer some service to her, like cleaning up a section of a beach you are familiar with or promoting a project. Or you may be willing to create a song, poem, or painting that honors the water. Leave the goddess with something tangible. Your gift could be the promise to visit a body of water and a guarantee that you will take a moment to send gratitude, love, and healing to that place.

When you are ready, you may return to this room and this place. Thank your helpers for their protection and guidance and close the portal with your intention.

Sharing

Pass the talking stick and have each member share their meditation experience.

Activity: Make Blessed Water at Your Altar

Go to your central altar, where you have set a bowl of water lined with crystals. Take a crystal or mineral wand and stir the waters as you read aloud:

> We offer prayers to Satet and Anket of Egypt, keepers of the water of the Nile, who are part of the triad with the ram god Khnum, who builds our bodies upon his potter's wheel along with our *ka*, our spiritual double. We offer prayers and gratitude to all the Celtic gods and goddesses of the waters. We honor all the keepers of the waters of the world. We give gratitude and pledge to support and clean the waters. We offer this prayer up in the name of the maiden, mother, and crone. We give our gratitude to the Great Mother Goddess and her many names. (Ask the participants to name other names for the Great Goddess. They can say the names out loud, popcorn style.)

After the invocation, have each participant take their turn stirring the water. As they stir, ask them to add their prayers of gratitude and love for the element of water, and to accelerate the vibration that the water holds for healing.

After each participant has stirred the water, give them a small vial and have them ladle some of the water into it. When everyone has their water, read the following lines out loud, having the participants repeat each line back to you:

> *We give our gratitude for the element of water.*
> *We vow to protect the water of our mother earth.*
> *We will do what is in our power to treat the water as sacred.*
> *With every shower or bath, with every dish washed, with every plant watered,*
> *We vow to express our gratitude*

For the live-giving, flowing essence of water.
And so it is!

When the ceremony is over, participants should take their vial of water with them. This blessed water should be added to a body of water for healing or can be poured down a drain to purify the system.

Sing

Choose songs that honor the element of water like "The River She Is Flowing" by Flight of the Hawk, or choose songs that honor the Mysteries. I suggest "There Is a Secret One Inside" by Kabir.

Sharing

Make prayers for the waters of the planet. Bless the west and tears and emotions. Bless all the mothers on the planet as well as the first mother. Bless the homelands.

What can we do to use less water, and to keep it pure? How can we work to protect the waters of our planet? Pass around the talking stick for ideas.

Pass out the prepared crane bags to your participants. These bags are inspired by Manannán mac Lir. He owned a magical crane bag which was blessed by his totem, the knowledgeable crane, a sacred bird whose wings made Ogham patterns when it flew. In your own crane bag, you can keep messages, small totems, and meaningful, spiritual power objects. Take a moment for each person to say a few words of hope and healing to energetically place in their bags. Encourage them to use their bags on their altars at home as they continue to fill them with important objects.

Ending

Release the goddesses. Close the portal, release the directions, and open the circle.

A Sea Story: Lineages, Water, and the Great Mother

Mor is all about our lineages. This includes our ancestral lines and the lands that we herald from. It also refers to our spiritual lineages: places and teachings around the world that we are drawn to. Mor is also about the waters on the planet, the Great Mother Goddess, and the feminine principle. This final ogham is about our own mothers and our female ancestors.

Our Lineages

Visiting the land of your ancestors is an amazing opportunity to find your own spiritual roots. I visited the British Isles in the early 1970s and loved it, although being in my early twenties, I hadn't read much about my homeland. I loved the tall standing stones placed in a circle around the meadows. They felt so important. I remember leaning against them and wondering what they were all about. This trip really acted as a beginning bookend for my work with the trees.

Since that time, I have sought out the traditional teachings of the Druids and the Celts and the ancient people of the British Isles. I wanted to reconnect with my ancestral roots. I refer to my ancestors as native European nature people. These are my relatives. They revered nature and gave their gratitude within the groves of their land. Trees were their teachers, as they believed that the tree teachings were expressions of divinity. These expressions were natural laws to live by. These people honored the Mysteries and revered the laws of nature that they held sacred. This interest has filled my life with deep meaning.

The bookend that caps my years of study, research, and ceremony was my trip to Ireland in 2019. I booked a three-week tour to connect with the spirits of the land. I just loved Ireland: the green, the drizzle and rain, the hills and mountains, the grazing sheep and cows, the ancient wells, the mysterious caves, the hidden fairy glens, and the ocean and lakes and rivers. There is a potent magic there, alive in the green. The otherworld sends messages through the weather and the birds. The unseen realm of the Fae is palpable. Most of all, I felt at home there. The people were funny and kind and generous. I believe that traveling to our root places helps us know who we are. It has certainly helped me.

I encourage you to find out more about the places your ancestors came from. Many folks these days are deeply interested in their genealogy, and I think this is a valid way of connecting with your roots. Websites such as Ancestry.com or DNA testing are ways to find out more. Finding out about your roots is one way to learn more about yourself. Browse the internet and read books about the history of the lands that you herald from. Perhaps one day you will arrange a visit. If you still have family elders in your life, set up some time to interview them about your family history.

The Wisdom Keepers

Most of us will identify with places around the world that we feel spiritually aligned with. It is the indigenous people of the globe that have held on to the knowledge and teachings of the original people who made these places their home. Fortunately for us, there are indigenous teachers and many books and sites that share this knowledge. Many indigenous people help with healing all around the world, and they provide us with experiences that let us know that reality is far more mysterious that we could ever fathom. This is a gift to us and helps us expand our consciousness.

Please think about supporting these wisdom keepers and their teachings by providing monetary support and prayers of gratitude. There are many wisdom keepers that share the ancient folklore and teachings of the British Isles. I have been lucky to meet a few of them and am ever grateful.

Our Spiritual Lineages

I encourage you to research places that interest you. Follow your heart with this. You may be attracted to Australia and the Aborigines, the Native Americans of North America, or the native shamans of South America. Most of us are interested in certain places like Peru, Egypt, China, Japan, or Africa because they have distinct cultures, histories, and long traditions of religions or spirituality. Each of these countries has "thin places," revered areas that are known for their high spiritual vibrations.

I encourage you to find out which religion or spiritual lineages you relate to. Find out something about another teaching besides the one you practice. Take a look at another religion, perhaps Hinduism, Islam, Christianity, Buddhism, or Paganism. Study shamanism of plant medicine in the mountains of the rain forest in South America or the teachings of Hawaii or Africa. Find out about holy places around the globe where you will find shrines, temples, and other powerful sites. Please be respectful. Do not usurp the spiritual practices of an indigenous culture that you study. If you choose to study in depth, I ask that you find a respected teacher that can guide you.

Allow yourself to explore your own spiritual interests. A spiritual lineage that I have investigated is Egyptian spirituality. I have traveled to Egypt eight times and have led three tours there. I have deeply enjoyed learning about the temples, sites, and tombs, and I have benefited from many blissful experiences encouraged by the Egyptian spiritual technology that is built into those places. I was blessed with a powerful teacher who accepted me into her lineage, but it still took years of study. It was only after a lot of preparation and many visits that I took on the special honor of leading ceremonies and rituals in the temples and tombs. I know this has been a great privilege and I am beyond grateful. For the last few years, I have been learning about the hieroglyphs, for no other reason than it makes me happy.

When I think about my work with the trees, I realize that I did not have a human teacher. I live in the Pacific Northwest in the United States, and I didn't know anyone else who worked with tree energy or who knew anything about the traditions and folklore of the British Isles. I learned as much as I could about each tree of the Ogham and slowly began to familiarize myself with the gods, goddesses, stories, and legends. Mostly, I learned from the telepathic messages that I received from the trees while working with them in ceremony and through guided meditations. I do claim my lineage to the British Isles and my connection to the land there, but what I share with you in this book is a result of my own experiences. I had no auntie, grandma, or elder to instruct me. Alas, my teachers came through the ether. This may be true for you as well.

The Water

Besides the themes of familial roots and spiritual roots, Mor is also about the water on the planet. We are reminded to be grateful for this gift and to work toward restoring all the water to purity. Give gratitude for the water that comes out of your tap. For the oceans, the seas, the rivers, the steams and brooks, the lakes and pools, the precious rain, and the water cycle. For the glaciers and the mountains that trap snow in the winter so that it runs into our water sources when the ice melts. There is so much magic built into the way our planet works. Water is a precious resource, and it requires our protection.

Offer your monetary support for organizations that are working to protect the waters. Offer a ceremony of gratitude for the water. Offer your time to a project. Cut back on your own water usage. Say a blessing of gratitude for water whenever you use it. The book *How to Create Sacred Water: A Guide to Rituals and Practices* by Kathryn W. Ravenwood is a wonderful source for creating crystal homeopathic elixirs to cleanse bodies of water both near and far. Research ways you can protect water sources and share what you learn. Learn how to help others around the globe that do not have fresh water. Find one thing that you can do to help with this.

The Mothering Principle

Finally, Mor is about the mothering principle. Here we honor the feminine principle and all mothers. We protect life and honor diversity. We take care of what we are given, we cooperate, and we share. We protect and nurture. Send some love to your female ancestors and to the women in your family. New mothers especially need physical and emotional support from their families, friends, and communities. Mothering an infant is especially draining. Women require renewal at all levels, and all mothers could use some help. This is true of childcare workers as well.

Mor is also about the blood mysteries of women and the moon's monthly shapeshifting. She is reflected light. She begins in the dark. She is the maiden, mother, and crone. Mor is the ability to create life. Mor is the mystery itself.

Forgiveness

The Great Mother is all about unconditional love and forgiveness. Undoubtedly, you have people and situations in your life that have wounded you, and it is true that forgiveness can set you free. Set your intention upon compassion and, when you are ready, allow forgiveness. If you are unable to forgive, you can ask the Great Mother to forgive through you and for you. I have experienced some amazing results when I worked with the Great Mother Goddess in this way. When I asked the Goddess to help me forgive a family member who harmed me badly, I found that the knot in my heart softened, and I noticed that this person was no longer on my mind. This felt rather miraculous after years of feeling haunted by their harmful actions. And I did not have to confront this member of my family in person. With that being said, I want to remind you that forgiveness is never something that you *have* to do. It truly is for yourself and your own well-being.

The Great Mother is a concept that lives in each person's consciousness at the personal and cultural level. This basic and fundamental expression of unconditional love and compassion lives in all of us. This practice can be used to forgive others and to forgive yourself. If the idea of working with the Great Mother and forgiveness appeals to you, here is the practice:

1. Decide that you want to forgive for your own peace of mind and well-being.

2. Intend to forgive. You don't have to know how you are going to do this.

3. Ask Universal Mind, Source, love, or a deity (like Brigid, Danu, Kuan Yin, Isis, or Hathor) to love through you. The Great Mother has no problem loving everyone. You can say, "The Great Mother loves through me. The Great Mother loves (the name of the person or situation you seek to forgive or your name) through me." The Great Mother will open you to this healing and express healing and forgiveness through you.

4. Be open and willing to receive guidance. This could come from any direction. Know that insight will be offered in a safe and healing way for all involved, including you. There is nothing else you must do.

We all have family stories, and some of us can go back many generations with written histories or oral information. Our personal stories wrap around our cultural stories and our past lineages and homelands. And we know that our world history is one of suffering. I also count the lineages and homelands from past lives through reincarnation; perhaps this explains why we are drawn to certain places and cultures. We are part of the past, present, and future, and we know that our world history is one of suffering. It is clear that within our stories is a great need for healing, reparation, and forgiveness. One person doing this work on themselves can heal generations and lineages. That is why it is so important and transformative. Painful as this work may be, I commend all of us who are actively engaging in forgiveness.

The Celtic Cosmology

I imagine that one of the reasons you picked up this book is because you are interested in the Celtic cosmology like I am. If so, I encourage you to immerse yourself in the sea of Celtic tradition. Read up on some of the Irish, Welsh, Scottish, and British stories and mythologies. *The Mabinogion* includes eleven medieval Welsh tales and is a good resource. Enjoy the Celtic gods and goddesses and reconnect with the sun, the moon, and the stars. Deepen your connection to fire, water, air, and earth. Surround yourself with animals, trees, and plants. Connect with the sacredness of nature and look to the enchanted springs and rivers, sacred groves, fairy mounds, and other portals to the otherworld. Consider the door named death and the afterlife.

When you investigate the Mysteries, it can be an awesome journey of self-discovery. Some of the fairy dust and mystery rubs off on you. You find that *you* are the mystery, and all of it lives within you. Enjoy the magic. I think it is this magic that is so attractive. Remember that we are all made of stardust. As such, we long to connect with the

Mysteries. We want to have our very own experiences with the other-world of fairies and unicorns, gods and goddesses, and our ancestors. We want to connect to our creator and our source. And we can!

I encourage you to bathe in the deep recovery of your own roots. Life is for learning, so do some research and study. Allow yourself new experiences as you reach out to learn about other ways to live, to pray, and to revere the sacred. Go into the forest and breathe. And mother yourself well—you are precious, indeed.

CONCLUSION

When I completed the first draft of this book, it just so happened to be Earth Day 2020, its fiftieth year. This day represents the environmental movement of everyday people acting with hope to change the trajectory of human impact upon the planet. The synchronicity gives me pause.

As I worked on my final edits in July 2021, we were moving past lockdown and mandatory mask wearing, which helped prevent the spread of the COVID-19 virus in the community. Many of us had gotten vaccinated; I did. Yet I doubted that we were done with this virus. It was a worldwide event, and we have seen so much death since March 2020.

This virus stopped human activity for a while. This allowed time for nature to take a break from the human impact that is global warming and climate change. We have seen that wild nature knows how to reclaim herself. From Yellowstone Park to South Korea to the ozone layer, we found ourselves witnessing what most of us thought only a faint possibility just a little while ago. In the near absence of human activity, the regeneration of Earth was vitalized and we began to see nature making a comeback. Having more impact than any policy or global treaty, humanity's global footprint has been radically reduced by simply slowing down, staying home, driving less, and consuming less. We have given our planet a rest. It is clear that the earth does not need us and, in fact, is endangered because of us.

It is my hope and prayer and dream that we can continue to find our way to environmental sustainability when and if things return to some sort of normalcy. I don't want to go back to the way things were. I believe that the answer for human survival lies in creating a simplified lifestyle that honors the planet. I hope that we can reach way back into history and call forward the wisdom and modeling of the ancient ones, the wisdom of our ancestors. We need to create a model for living that builds a thriving future for the next seven generations of humanity and all life on Earth.

Thank the Goddess for our indigenous cultures that based their economies and structures upon the principles that honored life through the practice of harmonious living with animals, water, soil, plant life, the elements, and the cosmos, none of us separate within the web of life. They are still with us, as are their teachings and practices. This is part of the reason why I share these ancient teachings from the British Isles.

The hope people have for creating a green economy and for producing green energy is not our way out. If you look deeply into solar panels, wind turbines, and the burning of biomass you see that there is nothing new here, and that money and environmental havoc are still running the show. Burning trees just exchanges one natural resource for another. All of these ways of creating energy still depend on oil and natural gas. And we need the trees for our oxygen, not to create more carbon dioxide by burning them.

What is required is a change of attitude, a change of lifestyle choices, and a great turnaround in accessing our place in the world and why we are here. For us to survive, we need to use less energy. We need to stop polluting the environment. We need to make better choices about what we buy. We need to become conscious about what systems we want to support. We need to support new technology that is not harmful. We need to back solutions that protect our planet, support the life of the flora and fauna, and return us to a sense of responsibility and humility.

Global warming and the impact of climate change are here. And humanity is getting a big wake-up call. We must stop. The virus stopped us, but just for a while. We are experiencing extreme heat and cold patterns, droughts, fires and smoke, monsoons with flooding and landslides, and terrifying super storms, hurricanes, and tornadoes. Although this is challenging and scary, we can look back to the ancient people when they faced a cold, dark winter. They adapted. They stored their food. They shared with their neighbors. They respected their water sources. They used only what they needed, and their needs were simple. It may be that we will have to totally let go of this modern lifestyle.

I don't know what is going to happen. We have such great challenges before us with this worldwide pandemic and the consequences of climate change. I believe our planet will survive and thrive without us. But it is my hope that we can come together as one global family and that we can build new systems based on equality, shared resources, and shared power—systems that treat the earth with respect and reverence.

There seems to be something about human nature that prevents us from knowing how to curb our desires; we will use and use until there is nothing left. There seems to be something about human nature that finds it easy to deny the fact that we are fouling our very own nest. I am surprised that the greater power that I call Source or Universal Intelligence has not given up on us. Indeed, this loving intelligence is still supporting us. The love is still here.

I hope that people will remember what our ancestors knew and built their lives upon: it is a sacred privilege to be born into this paradise, and our main job is to steward the water, the earth, and the air. Humans have forgotten that all living creatures are sentient beings and that everything on the planet holds a resonance and a spirit. All of these spirits have something to teach us and are worthy of our respect. The jury is still out on what the outcome will be for our species.

It is my hope that this book on tree teachings will touch your heart in a hopeful way. Go sit with a tree that you live close to and listen deeply to the counsel of that tree spirit. You will find courage and explore new ideas of how to proceed. Humans are such an amazing species, although so flawed. Let's move forward with humility and gratitude for the natural world that supports us. Stop and think about what you really need. Stop hoarding resources. Think about one another. Follow the golden rule—Are you treating others as you would like to be treated? Commit to becoming your best, wisest human self that partners with nature. Give back.

In great gratitude, I thank the teachings from the Celtic tree Ogham that I have included in this book, which add so much to the greater Celtic cosmology. I thank the Silver Fir and Pine, the Gorse, the Heather and the Mistletoe, the White Poplar and Aspen, the Yew, the Grove, the Spindle, the Honeysuckle, the Beech, and finally the ogham of Mor, which connects us to our maternal links. I hope their collection of teachings has added to your spiritual toolbox and inspired you as they have me.

I end this book with love for the reader and for all life on our great Mother Earth. Thank you for taking the time to read about these last ten ogham. Thank you for all that you do. I am thrilled that you love the trees and have given them your attention just by reading this book. And so it is.

APPENDIX A
Music

I have learned many songs in women's circles that I have participated in for years and I am not sure of their origin. Many I have learned from CDs and tapes, and you can find the albums on the internet to stream or purchase. I have placed an asterisk next to those that I think will be most helpful. They are excellent sources. If you want just one song, many can be streamed or purchased on various platforms.

Albums

Ani Williams, *Children of the Sun, Magdalene's Gift, Song of the Jaguar,* and *Wind Spirit*

Ani Williams and Lisa Thiel, *Sisters of the Dream*

Brooke Medicine Eagle, *For My People* and *A Gift of Song*

*Charlie Murphy and Jami Sieber, *Canticles of Light*

Danean, *Fire Prayer*

David and Steve Gordon, *Misty Forest Morning*

Dawn L. Ferguson, *Heartsongs of the Universe*

Enya, *The Memory of Trees*

*Flight of the Hawk, *Shamanic Songs and Ritual Chants*

Florence Lorraine Bayes, *In All Her Fullness*

*Jennifer Berezan, *Praises for the World*, *ReTurning*, and *She Carries Me*

*Libana, *A Circle Is Cast*

Lisa Thiel, *Circle of the Seasons* and *Invocation of the Graces*

Medwyn Goodall, *Medicine Woman*

*Moving Breath, *She Changes: A Collection of Songs from Healing Circles*

Performers at the Women of Wisdom Conference in Seattle, *Women of Wisdom*

R. Carlos Nakai, *Earth Spirit*

*Reclaiming and Friends, *Chants: Ritual Music*

Robert Gass and On Wings of Song, *Ancient Mother*

*Shawna Carol, *Goddess Chant: Sacred Pleasure*

Suggested Songs

Here is a list of songs and ways that you can find them. It is to your advantage to look up the words in advance and to make copies of the lyrics to pass out at your circles and ceremonies. You can look them up on the internet by title or author or by the album mentioned. You can also look up women's circle songs, Pagan songs, and nature songs.

For Calling In Spirit

"Listen, Listen, Listen to My Heart Song" (by Paramahansa Yogananda)

"O Great Spirit" (on the *Shamanic Songs and Ritual Chants* album)

"Oh, Great Spirit" (inspired by a chant by Adele Getty)

"Spirit Medley" (on the *She Changes* album)

For Creativity

"A River of Birds" (on the *A Circle Is Cast* album)

"Spiraling into the Center" (by Lorna Kohler)

"We All Come from the Goddess" (on the *She Changes* album)

For Honoring the Ancestors

"Blood of the Ancients" (by Ellen Klaver)

"Old Ones Hear Us" (on the *She Changes* album)

"We Are the Old Ones" (on the *Shamanic Songs and Ritual Chants* album)

For Honoring the Earth

"All My People" (by Brooke Medicine Eagle)

"Mother I Feel You" (on the *A Gift of Song* album)

"Where I Sit Is Holy" (by Adele Getty)

For Honoring the Goddess

"Blood of the Ancients" (by Ellen Klaver)

"Changing Woman" (by Adele Getty)

"Triple Goddess Chant" (on the *She Changes* album)

"Isis Astarte Diana Hekate" (by Deena Metzger and Caitlin Mullin)

"She's Been Waiting" (on the *She Changes* album)

"Spider Woman / She Changes" (on the *She Changes* album)

"The River Is Flowing" (on the *Shamanic Songs and Ritual Chants* album)

"We All Come from the Goddess" (on the *She Changes* album)

For Honoring the Mystery

"O Great Spirit" (on the *Shamanic Songs and Ritual Chants* album)

"Oh, Great Spirit" (inspired by a chant by Adele Getty)

"Sweet Surrender" (on the *Shamanic Songs and Ritual Chants* album)

"There Is a Secret One Inside" (from the poem by Kabir, translated by
   Robert Bly)

"Where I Sit Is Holy" (by Adele Getty)

For Honoring Trees

"Oh, Cedar Tree" (by Pauline and Joseph Hillaire)

For Meditating

"Light in the Mystery" (on the *She Changes* album)

"Song of Remembrance" (on the *She Changes* album)

For Honoring the Elements

"Earth Our Body" (on the *She Changes* album)

"The Earth, the Air, the Fire, the Water" (on the *A Circle Is Cast* album)

For Healing

"Old Ones Hear Us" (on the *She Changes* album)

"Song to the Mother" (on the *Fire Prayer* album)

"Spirit Medley" (on the *She Changes* album)

Ending Songs

"May the Circle Be Open" (traditional chant)

"Merry Meet" (traditional chant)

"We Are a Circle" (by Rick Hamouris)

For the Last Ten Ogham

Ailim/Silver Fir/Pine

"Light Is Returning" (on the *Canticles of Light* album)

"Sacred Ground" (by Brooke Medicine Eagle)

"Old Ones Hear Us" (on the *She Changes* album)

Ohn/Gorse

"Mother I Feel You" (on the *A Gift of Song* album)

"Oh, Great Spirit" (inspired by a chant by Adele Getty)

"Spirit Medley" (on the *She Changes* album)

Ur/Heather and Mistletoe

"Sacred Ground" (by Brooke Medicine Eagle)

"Sweet Surrender" (on the *Shamanic Songs and Ritual Chants* album)

"We Are One with the Infinite Sun" (traditional chant)

Eadha/White Poplar/Aspen

"Om Tare Tuttare Ture Soha" (traditional chant)

"The Earth, the Air, the Fire, the Water" (on the *A Circle Is Cast* album)

"We Are the Old Ones" (on the *Shamanic Songs and Ritual Chants* album)

Ioho/Yew

"Light Is Returning" (on the *Canticles of Light* album)

"Sacred Ground" (by Brooke Medicine Eagle)

"Old Ones Hear Us" (on the *She Changes* album)

Koad/Grove

"Old Ones Hear Us" (on the *She Changes* album)

"Blood of the Ancients" (by Ellen Klaver)

"The Burning Times" (by Charlie Murphy)

Oir/Spindle

"Sweet Surrender" (on the *Shamanic Songs and Ritual Chants* album)

"The River Is Flowing" (on the *Shamanic Songs and Ritual Chants* album)

"We All Come from the Goddess" (on the *She Changes* album)

Uilleand/Honeysuckle

I really like to use the poem "The Charge of the Goddess," which can be found online, or the song "She Who Hears the Cries of the World" by Jennifer Berezan. These are such excellent invocations for calling on the Great Mother that I highly recommend them.

"Sacred Pleasure" (on the *Goddess Chant* album)

"The Earth, the Air, the Fire, the Water" (on the *A Circle Is Cast* album)

"We All Come from the Goddess" (on the *She Changes* album)

"Where I Sit Is Holy" (by Adele Getty)

Phagos/Beech

"There Is a Secret One Inside" (from the poem by Kabir, translated by Robert Bly)

"The River Is Flowing" (by Diana Hildebrand-Hull)

"We All Come from the Goddess" (on the *She Changes* album)

Mor/Sea

"The River Is Flowing" (by Diana Hildebrand-Hull)

"We All Come from the Goddess" (on the *She Changes* album)

"We Are the Old Ones" (on the *Shamanic Songs and Ritual Chants* album)

"Where I Sit Is Holy" (by Adele Getty)

APPENDIX B

The Ogham of the Celtic Tree Alphabet

The Feada

#	LETTER/OGHAM	TREE/ MEANING	DATE(S)	TOTEM(S)
Aicme Beith				
1	⊢ B/ Beith	Birch/ Beginning	Nov. 1–Nov. 28	Snake, phoenix, eagle, falcon
2	⊨ L/ Luis	Rowan/ Protection	Nov. 29–Dec. 26	Horse, centaur, wounded healer Chiron
3	⊫ F, V, GW/ Fearn	Alder/ Guidance	Dec. 27–Jan. 23	Wren, raven, blackbird, crow, kingfisher, dragon
4	⊨ S/ Saille	Willow/ Feminine Principle	Jan. 24–Feb. 20	Bee, dove
5	≣ N/ Nuin	Ash/ World Tree	Feb. 21–Mar. 20	Dolphin, the Hanged Man tarot card, mermaid, water nymph

#	Letter/Ogham	Tree/ Meaning	Date(s)	Totem(s)
	Aicme Húathe			
6	⊣ H / Huathe	Hawthorn/ Cleansing	Mar. 21–Apr. 17	Fairy, the white stag, unicorn
7	= D/ Duir	Oak/ Strength	Apr. 18–May 15	The white stag, bull, rabbit or hare
8	≡ T/ Tinne	Holly/ Justice	May 16–Jun. 12	Swan, the Lovers tarot card, Castor and Pollux or Polydeuces
9	≣ C/ Coll	Hazel/ Intuition	Jun. 13–Jul. 10	Tortoise, turtle, crustacean, salmon, scarab, hare
10	≣ Q/ Quert	Apple/ Choice	Jun. 13–Jul. 10	Fairy
	Aicme Muin			
11	⟨ M/ Muin	Vine/ Prophecy	Jul. 11–Aug. 7	Lion, fairy, sylph, nymph, elf
12	⟨⟨ G/ Gort	Ivy/ Labyrinth	Aug. 8–Sept. 4	Spider, wolf
13	⟨⟨⟨ Ng/ Ngetal	Reed/ Direct Action	Sept. 5–Oct. 2	Owl, pike
14	⟨⟨⟨⟨ SS, ST, Z/ Straif	Blackthorn/ Negation	Sept. 5–Oct. 2	Birds associated with death, such as the vulture
15	⟨⟨⟨⟨⟨ R/ Ruis	Elder/ Renewal	Oct. 3–Oct. 30	Crane, stork, ibis

#	Letter/Ogham	Tree/ Meaning	Date(s)	Totem(s)
		Aicme Ailim (Vowels)		
16	╈ A / Ailim	Silver Fir/ Foresight	On Jan. 1 or post–Winter Solstice	Eagle, owl
17	╪ O/ Ohn	Gorse/Furze/ Collecting	Spring Equinox or Lammas	Bee, magpie
18	≣ U, W/ Ur	Heather/Mistle-toe/ Healing	Summer Solstice	Bee
19	≣ E/ Eadha	White Poplar/ Aspen/Adversity	Fall Equinox	Horse, white stag
20	≣ I, J, Y/ Ioho	Yew/ Rebirth	Winter Solstice	Raven, crow, owl, vulture, snake

The Forfeda

#	Letter/Ogham	Tree/ Meaning	Date(s)	Totem(s)
21	✕ EA, CH, KH/ Koad (Shears)	The Grove/ Temple Silence, Intuition	The Day, Oct. 31	Personal totems, owl
22	◇ OI, TH/ Oir (Helmet)	Spindle/ Fulfillment	Imbolc, Feb. 1	Thunderbird
23	⋉ UI, PE, P/ Uil-leand (Bones)	Honeysuckle/ Seeking	Anytime	Lapwig or peewit, hummingbird, bee, moth
24	ҏ IO, PH/ Phagos (Hook)	Beech/ Generations	Lammas, Aug. 1	Owl, snake, Tree of Knowledge
25	⊞ AE, XI, X/ Mor (Weft of the shirt)	The Sea/ Journey, Maternal Links	Anytime	Water nymph, mermaid, water creatures (dolphin, whale, salmon)

BiBLiOGRAPHY

Andrews, Ted. *Enchantment of the Faerie Realm: Communicate with Nature Spirits and Elementals*. Woodbury, MN: Llewellyn Publications, 2008.

Beresford-Kroeger, Diana. *To Speak for the Trees: My Life's Journey from Ancient Celtic Wisdom to a Healing Vision of the Forest*. Toronto: Random House Canada, 2019.

Budapest, Zsuzsanna E. *The Grandmother of Time: A Woman's Book of Celebrations, Spells, and Sacred Objects for Every Month of the Year*. San Francisco: HarperOne, 1989.

———. *The Holy Book of Women's Mysteries: Feminist Witchcraft, Goddess Rituals, Spellcasting, and Other Womanly Arts*. Berkeley, CA: Wingbow Press, 1989.

Cahill, Thomas. *How the Irish Saved Civilization: The Untold Story of Ireland's Heroic Role from the Fall of Rome to the Rise of Medieval Europe*. Vol. 5, *The Hinges of History*. New York: Anchor Books, 1995.

Conway, D. J. *Celtic Magic*. St. Paul, MN: Llewellyn Publications, 1991.

Forest, Danu. *Celtic Tree Magic: Ogham Lore and Druid Mysteries*. Woodbury, MN: Llewellyn Publications, 2014.

Gadon, Elinor. *The Once and Future Goddess: A Sweeping Visual Chronicle of the Sacred Female and Her Reemergence in the Cult*. San Francisco: HarperOne, 1989.

Gantz, Jeffrey, trans. *The Mabinogion*. London: Penguin Books, 1976.

Graves, Robert. *The White Goddess: A Historical Grammar of Poetic Myth*. New York: Farrar, Straus, and Giroux, 1978.

Hidalgo, Sharlyn. *Celtic Tree Oracle*. Victoria, Australia: Blue Angel Publications, 2017.

———. *Celtic Tree Rituals: Ceremonies for the Thirteen Moon Months and a Day*. Woodbury, MN: Llewellyn Publications, 2019.

———. *The Healing Power of Trees: Spiritual Journeys Through the Celtic Tree Calendar*. Woodbury, MN: Llewellyn Publications, 2010.

Jones, Kathy. *The Ancient British Goddess: Her Myths, Legends, and Sacred Sites*. Somerset, UK: Ariadne Publications, 1991.

Kynes, Sandra. *Whispers from the Woods: The Lore & Magic of Trees*. Woodbury, MN: Llewellyn Publications, 2006.

Kozocari, Jean, Jessica North, and Yvonne Owens. *The Witch's Book of Days*. Vancouver: Beach Holme Publishers, 1994.

Laxer, Judith. *Along the Wheel of Time: Sacred Stories for Nature Lovers*. Seattle: Booktrope, 2014.

Leek, Sybil. *A Ring of Magic Islands*. Garden City, NY: American Photographic Book Publishing Co., 1976.

MacEowen, Frank. *The Mist-Filled Path: Celtic Wisdom for Exiles, Wanderers, and Seekers*. Novato, CA, New World Library, 2002.

McColman, Carl. *The Complete Idiot's Guide to Celtic Wisdom*. New York: Alpha, 2003.

Murray, Liz, and Colin Murray. *The Celtic Tree Oracle: A System of Divination*. New York: St. Martin's Press, 1988.

O'Donohue, John. *Anam Cara: A Book of Celtic Wisdom*. New York: Harper Perennial, 2004.

Ravenwood, Kathryn W. *How to Create Sacred Water: A Guide to Rituals and Practices*. Rochester, VT: Bear & Company, 2012.

Starhawk. *The Spiral Dance: A Rebirth of the Ancient Religion of the Great Goddess*. San Francisco: Harper & Row, 1979.

Stein, Diane. *Casting the Circle: A Woman's Book of Ritual*. Freedom, CA: The Crossing Press, 1990.

van der Hoeven, Joanna. *The Book of Hedge Druidry: A Complete Guide for the Solitary Seeker*. Woodbury, MN: Llewellyn Publications, 2019.

Woodland Bard. *Bathing in the Fae's Breath: Boladh na Sióga within the Forests*. Ballinafad, County Sligo, Ireland: Bards in the Woods Media, 2015.

To Write to the Author

If you wish to contact the author or would like more information about this book, please write to the author in care of Llewellyn Worldwide Ltd. and we will forward your request. Both the author and publisher appreciate hearing from you and learning of your enjoyment of this book and how it has helped you. Llewellyn Worldwide Ltd. cannot guarantee that every letter written to the author can be answered, but all will be forwarded. Please write to:

Sharlyn Hidalgo
℅ Llewellyn Worldwide
2143 Wooddale Drive
Woodbury, MN 55125-2989

Please enclose a self-addressed stamped envelope for reply,
or $1.00 to cover costs. If outside the U.S.A., enclose
an international postal reply coupon.

Many of Llewellyn's authors have websites with additional information and resources. For more information, please visit our website at http://www.llewellyn.com.